THE **LINE** AND THE **DOT** ⋯ THE KINGDOM PIONEERS

PAUL CLAYTON GIBBS

BOOK **ONE** IN THE KINGDOM TRILOGY

THE LINE AND THE DOT: The Kingdom Pioneers
Copyright © 2010 by Paul Clayton Gibbs

Published by Harris House Publishing
Arlington, Texas
USA

Published in association with Pais Project Publications.

This title is also available in other formats.
Visit www.paisproject.bigcartel.com for ordering.

Requests for information should be addressed to: info@paisproject.com

Library of Congress Cataloging-in-Publication Data

Gibbs, Paul Clayton, 1964 -
    The Line and the Dot: The Kingdom Pioneers / Paul Clayton Gibbs
       p.cm.
    Includes bibliographical references
    ISBN 978-0-9824160-0-6 (pbk.)
    1. Christianity and Culture. 2. Christian Life. I. Title.
BR115.C8G53   2010
261 - dc22   2010925992

All scripture quotations, unless otherwise indicated, are taken from the Holy Bible, New International Version®, NIV®. Copyright ©1973, 1978, 1984 by Biblica, Inc.™
Used by permission of Zondervan. All rights reserved worldwide. www.zondervan.com

Internet addresses (websites, etc.) are offered as a resource to you. These are not intended as an endorsement by Harris House Publishing, nor do we vouch for the content of these sites.

All rights reserved. No portion of this book may be reproduced, stored in a retrieval system or transmitted in any form or by any means-electronic, mechanical, photocopy, recording, or any other-except for brief quotation in printed reviews, without the prior permission of the publisher.

Printed in Canada.

the team
author paul clayton gibbs
project manager terry tamashiro harris
dictation & research sebrina miller
editing & proofing terry tamashiro harris becca sherrill sebrina miller
design & typesetting paul green
publicity & promotion matt powell sam prescott

for lynn
my best friend
"number 9"

in memory of

doris || my mum who gave me the spirit of a pioneer — wish I had thanked you

my thanks to

joel || for being so easy to love. I pray you will see the pioneer I see and admire in you

levi || for being so easy to love. I pray you will know why you have so much creativity

dad || for being someone I could always trust, respect and want to emulate

harry || for being my pastor and letting me dye my hair red if I wanted to

pais || to my many friends who gave me a part of your life — it has been an honor

churches || sharon for pais' birth, thefaithworks for its incubation, pantego for its maturing

collective || for your belief in my *it*

sebrina || for your blend of gifts; we would be waiting another 8 years if it weren't for you

paul || for your inspiring commitment to our vision and the fun you bring to us all

mike and becca || for generously releasing me to write this book

terry and wayne || for making the book a reality

harris house publishing || for seeking God's Kingdom first and your business second

CONTENTS

prologue | 011

introduction | the spirit of the pioneer 019

stage one | revelation | my story 031
stage one | revelation | our story 047
stage one | revelation | your story 061

stage two | revolution | my story 071
stage two | revolution | our story 083
stage two | revolution | your story 104

stage three | resistance | my story 117
stage three | resistance | our story 135
stage three | resistance | your story 149

stage four | reproduction | my story 173
stage four | reproduction | our story 191
stage four | reproduction | your story 209

epilogue | 229

end notes | 233

PROLOGUE

PROLOGUE

5280

The Kingdom of God is 5280 feet long.

I love the cross. I love what it stands for. I love what it represents. I go to a church with crosses dotted all around. I know people who wear crosses around their necks. I sing songs about the cross. I hear messages from the pulpit about coming to the foot of the cross.

What is interesting is this: Jesus Christ never taught about the cross. He never mentioned the cross He would die on once...[1] But He does mention 'the Kingdom' *over one hundred times* in the New Testament.

The cross is vital to the message of Jesus but it is an invitation to something that goes beyond it. It is an invitation to be in relationship with God Himself through Jesus Christ—to be a part of the Kingdom.

As a Jew, Jesus was banned by religious law from saying God's name.[2] Instead Jesus used the word 'Kingdom' as a euphemism for God Himself. The word alone, however, also meant something very powerful.

Kingdom means *rule, reign, realm,* and *royalty*.[3] It is not a geographical place. You cannot find it on a map or a Sat Nav. It does not have a GPS or a map reference. It does not have a physical start and finish. But it is 63,360 inches long. Or if you're metric, it is 1069.44 meters long. Or if you lived in the days of the disciples, it is the length of 1000 paces.

The Kingdom of God is exactly one mile long.

impressment

Listen to these words of Jesus:

> You have heard that it was said, 'Eye for eye, and tooth for tooth.' But I tell you, do not resist an evil person. If someone strikes you on the right cheek, turn to him the other also. And if someone wants to sue you and take your tunic, let him have your cloak as well. If someone forces you to go one mile,

go with him two miles. Give to the one who asks you, and do not turn away from the one who wants to borrow from you.[4]

What exactly is Jesus saying here?

In the days of Jesus, the Jews believed God was going to set them free from the Romans. The Romans, of course, had other ideas. The Romans gave an element of freedom to everyone they conquered, but they used a tactic called *impressment* to remind their subjects who was boss.

Impressment was not meant to impress.

It was meant to intimidate.

Impressment allowed, among other things, a Roman soldier to conscript a Jewish native to carry his 100 pound backpack for one Roman mile.

The Jewish religious and political parties of the Second Temple period when Jesus lived had contrasting ideas of how to deal with the Romans. If you imagine it as a line, the different groups tended to sit at two extremes.

At one end sat the Sadducees and Herodians whose way was to give in and keep the party line. Although not necessarily happy with impressment, they would happily go along with a Roman to get along with the Romans. If it took one mile, then one mile it would be.

On the other end of the line were the Zealots and Pharisees whose way was to speak out and break the status quo. So unhappy were they with impressment, they would stir up trouble through violence or religious unrest. If they could avoid going the first mile, then no mile it would be.

The way of the first two groups meant they would *submit* to the world around them. The way of the second two groups led them to become *like* the world around them.

To those wanting to be part of His Kingdom, Jesus opened their eyes to a third way. His way would *change* the world around them.

Jesus impressed upon His disciples that in order to advance the Kingdom of God, they would have to relinquish the right to be part of a worldly system.

In the mind of Jesus...the Kingdom resides in the extra mile.

Many of us today wonder why we seldom see the Kingdom advance. We look around at society and our communities, and we rarely see the impact Jesus led us to believe could happen. Why?

celsius

Is it because we rely too much on the system? Doing what we *have* to do means we will just fulfill our duty. We will do what the rules, laws, and norms of the Christian life tell us to do.

But this only leads to maintaining the Kingdom. It is not advanced; it just treads water.

It takes an extra one degree to move a steam train.

Up to ninety-nine degrees Celsius and all you have is very hot water. There's a lot of energy, a lot of activity, but amazingly it is the one extra degree which creates the steam. The extra one degree takes a locomotive from being stationary to gaining traction, moving ahead, and accomplishing its purpose.

snip

On my journey and in the story that you're about to hear, I have discovered that the more I relinquish my rights and go the 'extra mile,' the more God can use me to make a difference in the world. We see the Kingdom come when we travel beyond the line on which so many sit, when we live in that extra mile.

Do you have a vision? Do you have a passion? Do you have a dream?

Then please understand that it is only in these 5280 feet that the Kingdom truly appears.

PROLOGUE

Jesus spent three years explaining how His dream would be pioneered, and He summed it up with a story of the third eunuch.

One day when the Pharisees approached Him in order to test him with a question about marriage and divorce, He gave this reply:

> For some are eunuchs because they were born that way; others were made that way by men; and others have renounced marriage because of the kingdom of heaven. The one who can accept this should accept it.[5]

In this simple statement, Jesus explains the three reasons humanity is the way it is: some were born that way and decide never to change; some were made that way by men and were molded by the people around them, allowing circumstances and situations to dictate who they should be.

But some had become who they are for the sake of the Kingdom of Heaven.

In the English language, 'sake' means *purpose* or *end*. In other words, Jesus is saying that those who want to pioneer the Kingdom on earth must put His purpose before their own, dying to their own rights. While many run after what they are not entitled to, Jesus' Kingdom requires a new breed of pioneers who will run *away* from what they *are* entitled to.

Now imagine yourself as a Roman soldier. You have been stationed in all different parts of the Roman world, and here you are in what is described as the armpit of the Empire. You have practiced impressment many times before. Most respond grudgingly. Occasionally, you found one or two who did not complain too much. Then one day this Jew, who calls himself a follower of Jesus, carries your backpack. After lugging it the required mile, he puts it down, looks you in the eye and asks, "Would you like me to carry it another thousand paces?" It is this act of going beyond that would see God's Kingdom revealed and perpetuated.

Jesus was, and is, looking to recruit a new kind of pioneer... Men and women who will leave their old ways far behind. Individuals who are so far beyond the line on which many others sit that the line is now a dot to them.

INTRODUCTION

THE SPIRIT OF A PIONEER

candle

It was my first trip overseas to share the vision of Pais. I'd been booked at a conference in Germany. For years I'd been praying I would be a person of influence, and here was my opportunity: two hundred youth leaders in one place. As I was shown to my hotel room, I asked my host who the other speakers at the conference would be. He replied, "It's just you."

I tried to act unsurprised.

You could say this was a step up for me. I had been ministering in schools mainly using simple object lessons to make the profound teachings of Jesus both simple and entertaining. My visual images stretched all the way from games to magic tricks. They were all packed into my suitcase, even my "magic candles". You know, the ones that relight after you blow them out? I had typically used them in elementary schools with the following script:

> "Jesus is the light of the world and He loves you, but what if you sin?"
>
> {Blowing sound}
>
> *Two or three seconds would go by then the candle would relight.*
>
> *The children would gasp.*
>
> "But His love never goes away."
>
> *I would repeat this alongside several reasons why God still loves us.*

The next morning as I was ushered into the conference room, the meeting's sense of expectancy was palatable. Ulle, my translator, had been a member of my first ever Pais team. As the conference host shared his vision for the two-day event, Ulle translated his words into English for me. Sometimes the speaker would go into less interesting, more practical logistics of the meeting. At this point she would cease to translate and I just looked around the room, smiling and wondering what was being said. Then it happened.

I noticed that after one thing he said, many of the people in the room surreptitiously took little glances towards me. I gently smiled back, slightly embarrassed but growing more curious. Waiting a few seconds, I turned and asked Ulle what he had said.

"Oh," she replied nonchalantly, "he's just said he believes that everything in German youth work in the last ten years has failed and that God has told him at this conference He will give him the vision for the future of German youth ministry."

"But I'm the only speaker?" I thought as I became gradually aware that in my folder, for that morning's seminar, all I had was my magic candle.

Sixteen years later, the Pais Project has put over a thousand full-time missionaries on four continents. But to grow Pais, I first needed to grow myself. I needed to more fervently embrace the spirit of the pioneer.

hebrews

Jesus longs for pioneers.

> *Do you see what this means—all these pioneers who blazed the way, all these veterans cheering us on? It means we'd better get on with it. Strip down, start running—and never quit! No extra spiritual fat, no parasitic sins. Keep your eyes on Jesus, who both began and finished this race we're in. Study how he did it. Because he never lost sight of where he was headed—that exhilarating finish in and with God—he could put up with anything along the way: Cross, shame, whatever. And now he's there, in the place of honor, right alongside God. When you find yourselves flagging in your faith, go over that story again, item by item, that long litany of hostility he plowed through. That will shoot adrenaline into your souls!*[6]

But what is a pioneer?

> *A pioneer is a person or group that originates or helps open up a new line of thought or activity or a new method or technical development.*[7]

A pioneer creates a path for others where none previously existed.

Imagine an old war movie where a small unit of soldiers must take the enemy's gun position.

A wall of barbed wire lies between them and their objective. So one of the soldiers, probably the bravest, runs out and throws himself upon the barbed wire. Lying fully stretched out on top of it, his body creates a path. The other soldiers then run single file across his back in order to gain the victory.

A pioneer does not simply *find* a way; a pioneer *becomes* the way.

John the Baptist was a pioneer. Jesus said of him, *"From the days of John the Baptist until now, the kingdom of heaven has been forcefully advancing, and forceful men lay hold of it."*[8]

The Kingdom broke through with John, not Jesus.[9]

When the church ceases to become a pioneering movement, it declines. When its members lose their pioneering spirit, they lose the power of spiritual progression. When the world loses the gift of God's pioneers, it loses hope.

My wife Lynn and I bought our first house in Moston, Manchester. It was never the nicest part of town, but it fulfilled our two requirements: it was close to the church and therefore within the needy area in which we wanted to serve. Our area had many problems. In fact, a national newspaper called the four streets that surrounded us "a ghetto of underprivileged underachievers". A year or two before the local government finally demolished the area, it sent a small pamphlet to fourteen thousand local residents. The pamphlet had a picture of a young boy named Robert. I would guess he was around age fourteen. It gave details of his ASBO (anti-social behaviour order) and listed the things he had done wrong and the nuisance he had caused. It showed a small map and told us where Robert was allowed to go and not to go. It listed the people he could not be with, and the family members he must be with if he was to step foot in his 'no-go zone'. It was probably the saddest piece of literature I had ever received through the mail.

There was a section entitled, *What You Can Do to Help*.

I thought, "Great! An opportunity, a chance, a way to make a difference. How can I serve? What's the answer?"

"If you see Robert[10] break his ASBO, please contact the police, or the Council's local housing service, safe in the knowledge that we will protect your privacy."

"Was that it?"

The pamphlet was two full pages, but I could summarize the whole thing in three words:

"We...give...up."

When the church gives up, when pioneers lose their spirit, hope is gone.

The Church, when it is advancing, is the one with the new ideas: hospitals, schools, orphanages...

But when the church stalls, it 'gets by' by copying the world's ideas.

The 'Christian version of' never works.

spirit

The spirit of a pioneer...

If Jesus could bottle it, He would.

There is a substance, a flavor, a zeitgeist a pioneer brings that a normal leader does not. Leaders are culturally relevant. Pioneers are culturally present.

There are several reasons why Jesus needs pioneers.

Pioneers inspire others. God used the stories of pioneers to call me to do what I do. It was the Hudson Taylors,[11] the Jackie Pullingers,[12] the Loren Cunninghams[13] of the world and their experiences which helped me realize I was shaped that way.

Stories inspire stories.

People listen to pioneers.

Let me ask a question: Who was the first man on the moon?

Neil Armstrong, right?

And what did he say?

"One small step for man, one giant leap for mankind."

Let me ask you another question: Who was the second man on the moon?

Buzz Aldrin, right?

And what did he say?

Who cares?!

Think about it. People who get asked the questions are often not the ones with letters after their names, but the ones who create something new. They are inventors of a new way of *thinking* or *doing*.

In 1972, NASA launched Pioneer 10, an exploratory space probe, with the primary target of reaching Jupiter.

Pioneer 10 surpassed expectations and its target, as Jupiter's immense gravity hurtled the satellite onward towards the edge of the solar system, passing Saturn and Neptune as well. Six billion miles from the sun, Pioneer 10 continued to beam radio signals to scientists on earth. And what was the most surprising thing? That signal emanated from an eight-watt transmitter as powerful as a bedroom night light and took nine hours to reach the earth. With a 'life' of just three years, Pioneer 10 kept going for over three decades.[14]

The signal of a pioneer lasts.

The signal of a pioneer is simply...

Their story and statement...

Such as:

Martin Luther King, Jr.: "I have a dream."[15]

Winston Churchill: "Never in the field of human conflict was so much owed by so many to so few."[16]

Jesus Christ: "I am the way, the truth, and the life."[17]

People are captured by the statement, but they *read* the story.

I truly believe that when the Church raises up pioneers, the world will come to hear what the Church has to say.

book

No longer can we dream dreams that are simply a cut and paste version of what is safe and familiar. Nor can we hope for that one-off event that provides us with a magic wand to life's issues. We must see vision as a certain process that goes beyond the system in which we presently live.

The Kingdom Trilogy book series is about going beyond in order to advance God's Kingdom. This first book, *The Line and the Dot,* equips Kingdom Pioneers; the second, *The Cloud and the Line*, examines Kingdom Principles. Whereas the second book suggests an alternative way of looking at morality, this first book proposes an alternative view of vision.

Why is it that so many individuals have come to me and shared their dreams, and yet so few have seen them realized? Maybe they never heard God in the first place. Maybe it was a human dream. Could it have been a figment of their imagination?

Or is there another possibility?

THE LINE AND THE DOT ⋅⋅⋅ INTRODUCTION

I have pioneered or re-purposed several things in my life, and over a period of time, I have realized there is consistency in the process. This book studies the four stages all pioneers inevitably go through:

> Revelation
> Revolution
> Resistance
> Reproduction

It also provides insight into the four major tests they will face:

> Loner
> Threat
> Conformity
> Authority

Throughout the book, I use the story of Pais as an illustration because its simple story clearly depicts so much of what I want to share.

Each stage is split into three sections:

> my story – *because it may not be the biggest or best story you will ever hear, but it is my clearest example*
>
> our story – *because we are all part of a connected story, and these sections will help you see the generic principles*
>
> your story – *because none of us can dodge the tests, but we can all pass them if we face the questions they ask of us*

To be forewarned is to be forearmed.

food

As I write, my family and I are enjoying watching Jamie Oliver's Food Revolution.

I have never related more to a TV program in my entire life.

If you have not already seen the program and would like to watch the dynamics of this book lived out in the comfort of your own home, then I highly recommend it. It is the story of an English chef who has come to the USA to challenge the food system of American schools. After a similar campaign in the UK, Jamie goes through the first two stages of pioneering just in the premier episode!

Hurdling obstacles such as "Who are you to come over here and tell us what to do?" and "That is Europe but this is America!", plus various concerns put forward to disguise the real challenges, I am convinced that this pioneer of healthy eating will go through the third and fourth stages as the series plays out.

I watch with anticipation yet feel that already I know the end of the story.

I sincerely hope that your story finishes well also, and that you press forward through each stage of pioneering to advance your God-given vision.

I hope this book equips you so that, rather than being surprised when certain things happen, you will understand it is simply a part of the journey. When you go through what all pioneers go through, I hope you will not be confused, think you have gotten it wrong, or worse yet, believe that God is no longer in control. Instead, my aim is that this book will both forewarn and forearm you with things I have learned along the way.

Finally, be strong in the Lord and in his mighty power. Put on the full armor of God so that you can take your stand against the devil's schemes.[18]

I pray for the hope of the world...those with the spirit of a pioneer.

STAGE ONE ✧ REVELATION

1

STAGE ONE

REVELATION | MY STORY

tent

The worst it ever got was when I asked my mother to tie me to the bed with my bandages. I was born with eczema, and by the time I was thirteen, the skin disease had become septic. My itchy skin would peel, revealing open, oozing sores whenever I removed my bandages. But this condition launched me on a journey I would never have fathomed, a journey which has led me to step foot in unexpected places, to speak to people I never imagined I would, and to share a passion I never dreamt I could have.

The first time I remember hearing about God was when I sat squirming in my chair with yellow pus on my arms and legs. I listened as my friends told me about 'The Tent'.

They had just come back from 'The Tent' and said it was only going to be there for a week. It had become a mysterious place in the minds of many of the young men in my boys-only school. The stories went something like this: people would go in, sing some strange songs, listen to a man talk, and then the man would pray for them. There was a bit of a buzz at the school because it was rumored that some of the boys who went had been healed. Sitting there in my seat, my friends simply said, "Why don't you go? You're practically a cripple."

I did not really believe in God, but didn't really *not* believe in God either. I had great parents, but like most young men in England at that time, I had not been brought up with a faith.

On the last day of 'The Tent', I went with my brother. I listened to the man speak, probably not understanding much at all. But something within me rose to the challenge of what he was saying. The guy, it turned out, was called an 'evangelist'. I wondered if that was his actual name. And then he tricked me.

He said a prayer and asked anybody who wanted to respond to say the prayer with him. And so I did it.

Then he said, "If you've said the prayer, put your hand up." Bemused, I did it.

He then said, "If you've got your hand in the air, please stand up." I found myself thinking, "One last thing and that is it." And so I stood. Then the sucker punch:

"If you're standing, please come to the back of the tent. I'd really like to talk to you."

Initially I did not get saved by Jesus; I got saved by a cute blonde. I was determined not to move, but the girl I'd been keeping my eye on throughout the service went forward, and mysteriously at that moment, I felt God call me too.

Something inside me thought, "If I do this, I might get healed." However, after a chat and a prayer, I went back into the main part of the tent to find everyone had gone. I left feeling strange and still itchy.

ferret

The first sermon I heard in church (two weeks after 'The Tent' and one week after my 14th birthday) told me I did not need a priest; I could pray directly to God. And so I did. One week later, my skin disease had gone. I remember thinking to myself, "If this is true, everyone needs to know about it."

Three years later, I had left church.

Five years later, I had left home.

Faith is an act of will, but I faithfully became willful. My belief never changed, but I did not want to live according to the boundaries set before me, and so I separated myself from anybody or anything that could tell me what to do. I ended up in a house made up of four apartments. In my apartment, I lived in with another apathetic and backslidden Christian. Opposite us were three very rich college students (one of them had a daddy who was the director of a world famous London department store). Above them were a hippy and a Jehovah's Witness. Above us were three anarchists and a ferret.

Now these anarchists were more than punk rockers; they were militant vegetarians. They would attack butcher shops in the middle of the night, gluing the locks and spraying "Meat means Murder" on the windows. Their vacations consisted of sitting down in the middle of a busy intersection and protesting. The house was full of all sorts of ideologies, arguments, and oxymorons. People whose lives contradicted their ideals. People like me. A punk postman who, despite being an anarchist, was by far the most ordered and self-disciplined amongst us. Poor little rich girls whose fathers' obviously felt that struggling through their student years was good for them. A Christian whose 21st birthday party resulted in one of his friends going into a drug-induced coma.

My beliefs never changed, but neither would they change anybody.

Roman, my best friend in the house (and an anarchist whose girlfriend was probably the most under-the-thumb woman I'd ever met), had no hope of convincing me of his politics. But neither did I, a man who was totally convinced that God was real and could heal, have any hope of convincing him of mine when he could see the lifestyle I'd chosen for myself.

In our entire house, the only one who was true to himself was the ferret.

witch

In the three years of life as a self-imposed spiritual recluse, I never spoke to another Christian. A couple of days after the birthday party, however, the police knocked on the door. The officer was someone I knew, a member of the small church I had gone to years earlier. Although we brushed him away, I could not brush away the presence he had brought into the house. That was the beginning of the end.

Only days later, on the top floor of a double-decker bus, I had a life-changing experience. From out of nowhere I was suddenly filled with hope and joy. There was no reason for it. I certainly had not summoned it up. It was just there. Then something inside me asked the question, *Do you remember this?*

I did.

The next thing I remember, I got myself back to church and on the back row made God a promise that I would return to Him.

REVELATION || MY STORY

Since the day of 'The Tent,' nothing had changed as far as the things I believed. In three years of not following God, it was a moving *away*, not a moving *towards* anything else. Even in those days, I told the members of the house, and many others, about this God who had healed me. And now as I was moving back towards Him, the desire to tell people about Him kept growing stronger.

When I was twenty-one years old, a friend told me of a two-week vacation on the streets of Edinburgh. I could be part of something called a 'mission'. I could tell my story for two weeks and even use my love for drama. It seemed to me I could become a kind of spiritual street performer.

One week into it, I knew what I wanted to do with the rest of my life.

I began to hear the term 'calling' spoken by various people. I was not sure what that meant, but I knew one thing:

This God I was learning about seemed very real, and if the stories were true, then the majority of people I met and knew had a very dark future, which frightened me more than it seemed to frighten them.

I had also heard the word 'missionary' and about an opportunity to train for four months to become one of them. It was an organization called Youth With A Mission which summed me right up. But there was a problem.

Her name was Lynn.

Someone had asked me if I believed there would ever be revival. I answered, "Yeah, sure," and jokingly said the sign will be when a girl with black spiky hair and big blue eyes walks into the church. I smiled wryly, doubting that day would ever come since I was the only 'post-punk' in the church. I spent my late teens shaving the side of my head, spiking my hair, and wearing black eye makeup. The chance of someone like me coming in was very, very unlikely.

But the unlikely sometimes happens.

On our first date we backed into a police car. It wasn't the best start, but we knew that we were serious about each other. Yet I was even more serious about this wild idea of being a missionary. I went off to train, knowing it would be the end of our relationship. We were still friends, and she occasionally visited me, but there seemed to be no future for us. Lynn knew that she was not called to Africa, Asia, or somewhere even more remote and desperate, but I was convinced that I was. Four months later, the same voice that said *Do you remember this?* said, *Go home to Manchester.* Confused as to why, I walked into my minister's office and asked if there was anything I could do for him. Unsure of where I was going, I needed to start somewhere and do something, and I knew going back to what I used to do was never going to be the right thing. It seemed that Lynn was right after all.

I would never *be* a missionary.

Instead, I would *make* missionaries.

My days consisted of typing letters, answering phones, visiting old ladies, and simply filling in gaps of day-to-day ministry. Every month I went with Harry, the pastor, to meet with a group of ministers. And that is where I heard about 'the witch'.

In England at that time, most of the 'men of the cloth' were given the chance to go into a local public school at Christmas and Easter to tell students about the festival they were supposed to be celebrating. Another guy named Paul had been doing this frequently, but then it happened.

A parent of two students, who happened to be a white witch, was opening an occult shop on the same road, and almost next to, where the tent had been placed. She kicked up a fuss in the local media about Paul's activities. They felt it was more of an advertising stunt for the shop than anything else. It made no difference. The doors of the schools shut. They shut tight.

baked beans

One day I got a phone call. A minister of a small youth group had some students who had been sharing their faith in their school, located in Blackley, which was around five miles from where I lived. Their strategy started very simply: a baked beans eating contest followed by an invitation to listen to their story. It went better than expected. Over the next few weeks, they retold their story to 20, 30, 40 students at a time every Wednesday during lunch.

But there was also a problem. The students would soon leave for college, so the lunch break activity would cease. The minister asked if I would meet with the school principal to see if I could carry on their work. I did, and not long after, untrained but undeterred, I was going in. I wanted to reach these young people in a way that made sense to them. A friend of mine, Paul Morley,[19] had taught me some simple presentation principles which I used and developed alongside other ideas.

Whenever I went into a school, I would look around and see several hundred students. My church youth group probably only had 20 to 30. And here was an organization called 'School' which had recruited 700 students and herded them into one building where someone else paid the gas, electric, and lighting bills.

Reaching into schools is not brain surgery. It's common sense.

I went to the Manchester Education Committee and asked for copies of their curriculum for certain subjects. One of the subjects was 'Personal and Social Education'. As I looked through the syllabus, topics popped out that shared common values with the message of Jesus [identity, purpose, direction, relationships]. So I went back to the school and approached the head of PSE.

"When you teach law and order," I said, "you invite the police in to speak. When you teach health and safety, the fire service is involved. When you teach these subjects, would you like me to provide a similar service? I could give examples, I could share stories, and I could bring a fresh voice."

During my time as a school pupil, I had learned a valuable lesson. In the religious education I'd received, I had two different teachers. They both taught about Christianity, but one turned me off of God, and one turned me on to God. The first taught the program. The second taught passion.

The head of PSE agreed and gave me opportunities to teach lessons. My first memory of ever being introduced in a school went like this:

"Students, as you know, we have been going through a series teaching the myths of the world, and last week we looked at the story of Noah's Ark. Well this week, we have found someone who actually believes that happened. His name is Paul Gibbs. Let's welcome him to the class."

In a fifty minute lesson, I spent half of it trying to explain the logistics of how Noah's Ark might have happened and the other half answering questions. Questions such as, "Have you always believed this?" and "Do your parents believe this?" Questions which led to answers such as, "No, but let me tell you about my skin disease…"

It is not our beliefs that transfer. It is our passion.

I have only been to one ice hockey game. I went with my two sons and a Canadian friend to whom ice hockey was a second religion. Three times a fight broke out on the ice. To me it looked a little like 'handbags at six paces' (an English expression that means the fight was a bit girly and staged). During the first fight, my sons and I were totally unmoved. We had a quick discussion with my friend who thought that the fights were just part of the game. During the second fight, my friend got quite excited. He could not help but shout encouragement to his team. I noticed my boys watching him. The third time he was on his feet cheering. My boys didn't stand, but they also cheered along.

Interesting, isn't it?

During all three fights, his beliefs never changed. But when he showed passion, my sons got excited and joined in.

It is not our beliefs that transfer. It is our passion.

snapper

I was never really a rebel at school, yet I often got into trouble. I was not mischievous, a trouble-maker, or what you might describe as particularly naughty…I was just living on a different planet from everyone else, a little unaware of the realities of life. It was a snowy day and I was fourteen. I walked out of class onto an empty playground.

The playground was L-shaped in a school made up of around 600 boys. I could not see a single one of them in my part of the L. However, I could hear a distant roar. I walked up the playground and around the corner, and there it was: the fight. A band of around 100 boys encircled what would be a traditional scrap, but as I got closer I realized that this fight was different. Rather than two young men fighting it out at the center of a human gladiator ring, there was one single person, an infamous teacher.

'The Snapper.'

That was what we called him anyway. He had a reputation for losing his temper and was one of three teachers known to have fights with the students. It was obvious now what had happened. He had been lured into a trap. The boys were threatening to throw snowballs at him or go after him in some way. He was gesturing that he would take us all on.

In my naivety, this seemed like fun. I picked up a snowball. When I say snow, it was a three part mixture of snow, ice, and grit. I threw it at the Snapper. It was the most perfect snowball throw I had ever launched. As it arced, it was as though everything went in slow motion. Every eye traced its trajectory. The Snapper looked up. His face slowly turned from anger to surprise to utter disbelief as the snowball exploded on the bridge of his nose.

Silence.

I realized I may have made a mistake when the circle parted with a deadly hush, allowing me to make my escape. I ran. The Snapper pursued me. I slipped. The Snapper kicked me in the head three times and ran off, looking back only once.

Going the extra mile means going beyond yourself, beyond what has already been achieved.

I walked into my old high school for the first time since leaving it seven years earlier. Just as I had looked around at the local school in Blackley and seen a need, so now I was looking around the wider community and seeing a greater need. I had established a good reputation in the Blackley area and had seen the benefit to the Kingdom. But the time had come to push beyond my comfort zone.

As I walked through the corridors to my appointment with the headmaster, I passed a teacher who looked at me with curiosity as if to say, 'I know you from somewhere.' We passed with a simple nod to each other, saying nothing. It was the Snapper. I was already nervous. This was the first new school that I had approached. I felt like turning around. I'm glad I did not.

Over the next couple of years, I built a relationship with many schools that I visited on a regular basis. At five of those schools, I ran a lunchtime club. At others I just taught lesson series on a regular basis. At still others I simply did the occasional lesson or assembly.

But then the questions came.

questions

Just over three years after the Baked Beans Gospel Mission, I was now serving around 17 schools and teaching 10,000 students per year. But certain things nagged away at me. There's a difference between making converts and making disciples, and as usual, the difference needed to come in me. This restlessness had been going on for some time, and then one day after teaching a lesson on some area of my faith, one of the students approached me.

"I love your lessons," he said. "In fact, because of your lessons, my parents want to know more, and so they've asked these two men to come to our house one evening a week."

This intrigued me. "What do they look like? Maybe I know them."

"They wear blue suits," the reply came. "And backpacks."

I felt a real sense of responsibility to the young people I was reaching. If they were simply numbers, they would look good on my resumé. But the Kingdom only advances in the extra mile. I needed to go beyond.

I had five questions gnawing away at me. Five questions I had no answers to.

Question One: How could I get these interested students discipled in their local church?

It was, and is, my belief that young people need to be part of the wider Christian community in order to grow spiritually. At fourteen, I had plugged into the local youth group, but not the rest of the church. At seventeen, when my peers left for college, my support system evaporated.

Question Two: How do I get more churches directly involved?

I was blessed to have as a pastor a man who lived what he preached. When he spoke about the Kingdom, he really meant it. While still paying me as his youth pastor, he saw a need in another church and asked me to serve their youth group, instead of ours, for an entire year. Here was a pastor who knew it was not about his church, or his empire, and that no one church had all the answers. I knew I needed far more churches involved if we were going to successfully serve the schools and the students of North Manchester.

Question Three: How do I help churches reach and keep students?

The things that *reach* people are not the things that *keep* them. The things that *keep* them are not the things that *reach* them. I could reach young people in schools, but on my own I could not help churches keep them. When a student would ask where they could find out more of what I was talking about, I would tell them about a church nearby and its youth program. But then the inevitable questions would come.

"Will you be there?"

The answer was always..."no."

Question Four: How do I keep the ministry fresh and varied?

We do not need heroes; we need heroic teams. Hollywood promotes heroes. Even some churches promote heroes. But God wants us to model community. Young people need to see how they can be part of a heroic team. No teacher, no matter how interesting, can present the fullness of God. It takes community.

I knew that a team displaying gentleness and respect to each other in the way they led an assembly or lesson or lunchtime club would have far more impact than the cleverest, most inspirational talk I could conjure up.

Question Five: How do I attract a large number of missionaries to help me in the vision?

Around that time, there were several internship programs, but they were often limited in numbers. Part of the reason for this was the cost to the recruit. The money they paid provided the salary of a person in charge of the group. I had a problem though. I was beginning to get the sense that I may need a lot of missionaries.

pais

After three years of questions and experimentation, Pais was founded in September 1992.

It was the best answer I could come up with.

Relationship, of course, is always the key. I had to develop a relational bridge between the school and the church.

The best way to do this, it seemed to me, was to recruit young people, train them, and then place them in churches that were nearby the schools. To get more churches directly involved, it had to be very low cost.

The first church to become involved only had about forty members. So rather than raising money to buy a house to put a team in, I asked the church if they could simply house and accommodate their intern with a family from the church. Not only did it keep the cost down, but this more thoroughly integrated the missionary into the church. That young person, trained by me, would fully engage and serve that Christian community in their youth ministry.

The idea was to help the youth group become a more relevant place for the non-churched to go to church.

That first year I travelled the length and breadth of Great Britain to find recruits. Ulle, a German young woman; Joanne, a Bible college graduate from the south of the country; Gary, a local youth pastor; Lisa, a high school graduate from Birmingham, England, and myself became the first team.

We were all based in different churches, but came together each morning at 8 o'clock to pray and prepare. During the week, we served the schools of North Manchester, building relationships with teachers by keeping within their boundaries and offering enthusiasm, passion, and professionalism. In the evenings and weekends, we served our different churches, coming alongside their youth pastors and other volunteers.

In answer to my final question, I felt God speak clearly to me…I would make Pais free and trust Him for the money needed to run the team. That first year every one of us grew. We saw many young people ask their questions, and their questions led them to our churches.

Pais was born, but it was still very small.

THE LINE AND THE DOT ⋯✧⋯ STAGE ONE

questions for the pioneer

1. What similarities do you see between my story and your story? Try not to look at circumstances, but principles.
2. Pick a section from *my story* and write down what you think I was feeling in that situation. If you had gone through the same situation, how would it have made you feel?
3. How do your feelings affect what comes next?

STAGE ONE

REVELATION | OUR STORY

revelation

When did Jesus know He was God?

Was He born knowing? Or at some point did He become aware? We do not really know the answer to this question. We have our ideas, but as with many things, we're not all on the same page.

Some think perhaps it was at His baptism.

> Then Jesus came from Galilee to the Jordan to be baptized by John. But John tried to deter him, saying, "I need to be baptized by you, and do you come to me?"
>
> Jesus replied, "Let it be so now; it is proper for us to do this to fulfill all righteousness." Then John consented.
>
> As soon as Jesus was baptized, he went up out of the water. At that moment heaven was opened, and he saw the Spirit of God descending like a dove and lighting on him. And a voice from heaven said, "This is my Son, whom I love; with him I am well pleased.[20]

Jesus was a pioneer, and as with all pioneers, the first stage is Revelation.

When God first gives vision, it is usually to an individual rather than a community. A pioneer is a person who is first given a vision and then made aware of God's thoughts or feelings toward something. Vision is possibly the greatest element of change we can experience.

33 1/3

Pioneers need a *bigger* vision. A bigger vision changes us. A bigger vision helps us to see ourselves as bigger people.

I was expelled from the first school I ever attended.

If this book ever becomes an audio book, the publisher will likely not want me to read it aloud. I was born with a slight speech impediment. Living in America is great because people think I'm just English. In reality however, I am afflicted with a mild form of dyslexia and often do not pronounce my words correctly.

So, when I was six years old, my parents sent me to a private school for elocution (diction), movement, and dance lessons. A short time later I was expelled... for biting the girls. My parents took me to a doctor who announced:

"Mr. and Mrs. Gibbs, your son is a problem child and always will be."

In high school, my nickname was 'thirty-three and a third'. I was told that my voice sounded like a single playing record, which runs at 45 RPM, being played at album speed...33 1/3.

I tend to slur my words. I never saw myself as a *public* speaker. And I certainly did not see myself as a *popular* speaker.

I never related well to young people, even when I was a young person. When teachers were late, which seemed to happen quite often, a cry would go out, "Let's crucify the Christian!" Everyone would cheer, including me. And then I realized: *I* was the Christian. In a class of thirty-five boys, I was the only Christian. After a short scuffle, one of two things usually happened. Either I would be buried under every single table and chair in the room, all piled on top of me in an artistic yet life-threatening manner, or alternatively, I would be hung from the high ceiling with the ropes that were usually used to open the top windows.

As I said, I never imagined I would be a public speaker or a popular speaker. But vision changes us. When we see a bigger God, we see a bigger God in us.

barbados

A *bigger* vision motivates the pioneer within us.

I love to surf, and so on the tenth anniversary of the Pais Project, I was incredibly excited when an offering was taken to give our family a month-long sabbatical. I bought my second favorite book, *The Stormrider Guide—The 80 Greatest Surf Spots in the World*. I tend to get obsessed with things, so for about three weeks, I read the book inside and out, coming to the conclusion that Barbados was the best place to go at that time of year. I absorbed every little fact I could. I knew the name of every single wave spot and if it was a beach break, reef break, or point break. I knew if the wave went left or right or both ways. I did not just look at the surfer on the front cover; I *was* the surfer on the front cover!

I went to the gym to get my body ready for my dream trip. On the first day, I set the treadmill for a fifteen-minute hill run, pressing the button so the ramp would rise to a 30-degree angle. Within about two minutes, I was gasping for air and counting down the time I had left. At the gym I attended, there were television screens in front of the machines. Normally, they were tuned to some dull sitcom or Oprah interviewing a man who had a sex change and was now called Brenda and was going to have a makeover and meet her long lost son flown in from Australia. On one particular day however, a TV screen about twenty feet to my right showed a surfing expedition. After five minutes of physical torture, I unplugged my ear phones, relocated to the machine in front of the screen, and set it with my fifteen-minute program.

The show was FANTASTIC! It was a documentary of five surfers who'd gone on a tour of Indonesia's best surfing spots. I got so into it that at one point, the surfer went left and so did I, falling off the machine with a crash. Embarrassed, I got back on and continued to run. Then the worst thing imaginable happened: my machine broke. Or at least it appeared to. When I looked down, it was flashing 'fifteen minutes'.

I had run the race but had not noticed the effort.

That is what vision does for us. When we lose vision, we notice the pain. It might be the pain of sacrifice, the pain of self-image, or the pain of self-doubt, but we notice the pain.

F1

Pioneers need a bigger vision *from* God. A bigger vision *from* God steers us. A bigger vision *from* God helps steer others.

I was watching an interview of Damon Hill, the British Formula One champion from the 1990's.[21] He was asked how he was able to drive around the corner at such huge speeds without hitting the curb. His reply was, "It's simple. You do not look at the curb; you look at the invisible, imaginary driving line."

When I was younger, my favorite computer game was a Formula One simulation. It had various settings of difficulty. The easy setting did not make the car go faster or the other cars go slower. It simply added a white dotted driving line. Hill is right—the minute you take your eye off the vision, and you try to avoid the curb, you end up hitting it. You either hit the curb or steer so far away to avoid it that you find yourself hitting the *opposite* curb.

The Pharisees had a similar problem. They believed the Messiah would come if the people of Israel cleaned up their act. The Pharisees' vision became *Let's Not Hit the Curb of Sin*. Instead they went the opposite direction and hit the parallel curb of *legalism*.

As a pioneer, the author of Hebrews teaches us that our vision must be nothing less than...Jesus. [22]

But where does revelation come from? Where do we get it?

How do we gain revelation? The passage in Hebrews which speaks to pioneers gives us some great advice: *Keep your eyes on Jesus, who both began and finished this race we're in. Study how he did it.*[23]

neighbor

Pioneers need a bigger vision *of* God. A bigger vision *of* God sustains us. A bigger vision *of* God helps us sustain the vision in others.

We do not need a vision of vision.

One of the possible reasons that so many visionaries fail is because they have a vision of vision. It is a building or a numerical goal, a project or who knows what. The problem with this is when the vision is going well, they are doing well. When the vision is going badly, they are doing badly. Their view of God and their view of how God sees them, indeed their very *intimacy* with God, are dependent upon external circumstances.

But God is a circumstance that never changes.

You can tell if a youth pastor has a vision of vision. On a Wednesday or a Friday night, they are incredibly passionate about their message. They are creative. They plead with the young people to hear the Word of God. But their next door neighbor does not even know they are a Christian.

A vision of vision is a *cut and paste* vision. A vision of vision gives you compartmentalized vision.

A vision of God, however, gives you a *theme*.

My vision is not the Pais Project. My vision is not a number. My vision is not a building. My vision is not even schools work. My vision is a theme, not a target.

My theme is to make missionaries. Whether I'm leading a church, parenting my children, heading up an international organization, or talking with a friend, my vision of God inspires me to make missionaries.

A vision *of* God creates a vision *for* God. The two are intertwined.

As you pioneer, I want to warn you not to fall into the trap of having a vision of vision. Instead, push beyond that simple and shallow motivating force. Wrestle with God until you have a vision of Him...of who He is—not just what He wants you to do, but why He wants you to do it.

Why would it please Him?

What is the bigger picture He sees that this is just a small part of?

This will not come quickly. This is not a shortcut. This is a long haul, and to be perfectly frank, sometimes a laborious path. In the end, however, both you and your vision will be sustainable. Furthermore, do not be surprised if your vision of God creates a theme within your life.

But where does revelation come from? How do we get it?

seed

When pioneers first receive a vision, it is not the finished concept. It is just a seed. A seed is not the plant. It does not taste like the plant, look like the plant, or feel like the plant. It contains within it, however, the potential to be the plant.

Another great story of Jesus the Pioneer occurred on the road to Jericho. (Or was it the road from Jericho? We will discuss that later.) As Jesus walked along, blind Bartimaeus, the son of Timaeus, called out to Him:

> *Son of David, have mercy on me!*[24]

Now this is an interesting thing for a beggar to shout out.

'Son of David' meant more than simply being a son of a man called David. It was a title—the title given to the One who would be known as the Messiah. The son of Timaeus, although blind, could see the Son of David. Others only saw the son of Joseph.

Bartimaeus saw with his own eyes the miracles *of* Jesus, but only after he saw with his real eyes the miracle that *is* Jesus.

For us to see, we first have to be blind.

A number of groups in Jesus' day were looking for the Son of David.

The Zealots thought the Messiah would be a militaristic hero. They believed if they could stir up Israel to fight the Romans, God would send the Messiah to free them.

The Essenes had given up on Jerusalem and the Temple and had run for the hills. They lived in a holy huddle, having nothing to do with the rest of the Jews. They had their own schools, their own shops...essentially their own community. They believed the Messiah would recognize that only they were the sons of light.

The Pharisees were looking for a Messiah sent by a Holy God. If they could only get Israel to clean up her act and eliminate the sinners, then surely God would send the Son of David.

One of the disciples many years later said something quite odd. He said that the true light that gives light to every man was coming into the world. He was in the world, and though the world was made through Him, the world did not recognize Him.

Perhaps the reason we fail to recognize God or a move of God in our lives is not that we do not know what He looks like, but that we have already decided what He looks like.

True pioneers are blind.

Vision should not come to the pioneer secondhand. For some, like a beggar, their visions are just scraps of food cast away by others. They live off the vision of a leader or a preacher or a TV star. Some beggars become thieves. We are not to do the same.

As a child in England, one of my favorite places was the Pic & Mix counter in the local supermarket. You could choose two or three sweets of one variety and mix them with three or four sweets of other varieties and have them weighed. For some, this is what makes up their vision.

Pioneers learn from other visionaries. We may benefit from their advice and even from aspects of their models and programs, but ultimately a pioneer needs to receive a vision from God.

But where does revelation come from? How do we get it?

300

Jesus asks Bartimaeus a question.

What do you want me to do for you?

Now to an average person, this seems like an unusual thing for Jesus to ask. Surely it is obvious.

Unusual? Yes. Uncommon? No.

Bible scholars estimate that Jesus was asked 300 questions during His ministry.

He gave a straight answer to three.

Interestingly, we can find where Jesus asked 125 questions. Many of these were *in answer* to questions He was first asked.

Jesus was a pioneer, but He was also a rabbi. Rabbis answered by asking.

Why?

Perhaps the best illustration of this is the true story of a tourist who was shopping in a photographer's gallery in Jerusalem. Finding it difficult to choose from all the beautiful photos, the woman decided to ask the Jew behind the counter a question.

"Which one is your favorite?"

He replied, "Are you married?"

Now you might have expected her to walk out of the shop without an answer, thinking the photographer was very rude or quite forward. However, she had been on a tour of the city and learned that a rabbi answered questions with a question. So instead she replied, "Yes...why?"

"Do you have children?" was the even more random response.

"Yes...why?"

"Which one is your favorite?" His third and final question contained the answer.

Now let me ask you a question. Whose answer was it? It was not simply his answer; it had become her answer. She owned the answer.

Vision comes from a conversation of awkward questions.

awkward

The greatest vision comes from the greatest questions. The biggest vision comes from the biggest questions. The simplest vision comes from the most awkward questions.

A revelation *is* a conversation of awkward questions. Think about it. Moses, Paul, even Jesus received vision from conversation. Mistakenly, we think Moses was given his vision from a burning bush. But the bush was not the vision; it simply caught his attention. His vision came from an awkward conversation recorded in Exodus 3. "I am sending you," says God. "Why me?" asks Moses. "I'm a nobody. I can't speak well. I don't know all the answers."

Saul of Tarsus, later named Paul who was the author of the majority of the New Testament, did not receive his vision from a blinding light. The blinding light took away his vision! The blinding light simply got his attention. His vision came from an awkward conversation.

> *"Why are you persecuting me?"*

> *"Who are you, Lord?"*[25]

I received my vision for the expansion of Pais during a thirteen-day conversation as I walked across England.

When the conversation stops, the vision stops.

Pioneer...what is getting your attention right now? What awkward questions do you have for God? Can I encourage you to ask them and keep asking them, but do not walk away when you are asked some awkward questions in return.

Jesus understood the need to ask questions even at twelve years old.

> *Every year his parents went to Jerusalem for the Feast of the Passover. When he was twelve years old, they went up to the Feast, according to the custom. After the Feast was over, while his parents were returning home, the boy Jesus stayed behind in Jerusalem, but they were unaware of it. Thinking he was in their company, they traveled on for a day. Then*

they began looking for him among their relatives and friends. When they did not find him, they went back to Jerusalem to look for him. After three days they found him in the temple courts, sitting among the teachers, listening to them and asking them questions.[26]

Three days.

Asking questions.

oneighty

In this long haul conversation of awkward questions, we can receive a bigger vision of God. This bigger vision will sustain us and keep us going. The bigness will create a theme for our life, not just a target.

A thematic vision outweighs a targeted vision. Not only does it last longer and go deeper, it is much wider. By this I mean a thematic vision encompasses the whole of our lives and our thinking. Everywhere we go. Everything we do.

On one of my earlier trips to the States before Pais was planted there, I was taken to see an incredible youth ministry building in Tulsa, Oklahoma. Oneighty is the youth ministry of a mega church.[27] My tour guide was excited for me to see it, and as we drove onto the campus I understood why. The building was huge. Not only huge, but the facility was cutting edge in everything from technology to design. The reception area was a work of art. The snack bar was clean and sharp, rivaling any cinema in the world. In between the reception and snack bar was a basketball half-court, entirely encased in glass. On the second level were rows of iPods (which were still a novelty at that time) alongside rows of the latest game consoles. There were cool breakout areas and a lounge that was five times the size of, and just as edgy as, Central Perk in *Friends*. Behind all this was the meeting room, or sanctuary as they call it, seating up to 1200 teenagers every Wednesday night.

The place was, as they say in America, *awesome*.

I continued on my road trip very excited. It was not so much the building that excited me. I have never really been impressed by large buildings. But the faith of these American Christians astonished me. What gave me so much hope was their belief that God could provide the huge amounts of money that such a facility required.

And so the thought that buzzed through my mind was simply this: Just wait until I tell them about schools ministry! Just wait until I explain that with Pais the churches in America can put full-time missionaries in local schools for relatively no cost.

When I showed the photos of Oneighty throughout England, the most common comment, accompanied by a wry smile, was: "Only in America."

Later on, as I began to speak to pastors in Texas, I waited for their eyes to light up as realization suddenly exploded in their minds that for the same amount they'd been spending on buildings, we could put thousands of missionaries into local schools.

And then it happened.

The wry smiles crept across their faces, and the words seeped out: "Only in England."

This is the problem with vision of vision. We believe that God is the God of the impossible in one area of our lives but not another.

In England, He is the God of the impossible schools outreach but not of the impossible building.

In America, He is the God of the impossible buildings but not of the impossible schools outreach.

A bigger vision of God helps us understand this: If God is God of the impossible in one area of our lives, He is the God of the impossible in *every* area of our lives.

With a thematic vision, we understand it is all or nothing. And usually we conclude that it is all.

questions for the pioneer

1. Please list your most awkward question for God and your most awkward question for yourself.

2. What captured your attention? What was your burning bush experience?

3. If vision comes through a conversation of awkward questions, in what practical ways can you keep that conversation going? Don't just think, *What different questions do I have?* Think, *What different ways can I ask those questions?*

STAGE ONE

REVELATION | YOUR STORY

loner

Just before Jesus hit the teenage years, He hit the first test of a pioneer.

> *Everyone who heard him was amazed at his understanding and his answers. When his parents saw him, they were astonished. His mother said to him, "Son, why have you treated us like this? Your father and I have been anxiously searching for you."*
>
> *"Why were you searching for me?" he asked. "Didn't you know I had to be in my Father's house?" But they did not understand what he was saying to them.* [28]

Every stage a pioneer goes through involves some kind of test. God does not protect you from these tests for an important reason which we will see later.

During the stage of revelation, the test you will face as a pioneer is the one of being a loner.

it

At this stage, simply put...

People believe in *you*, but they do not believe in *it*.

When you share your vision, please do not be surprised if those closest to you do not understand it. They may grasp aspects of your vision, but the things that make it unique will be the things that most confuse them.

When I shared the vision of the Pais Project, some of my best friends were my colleagues in ministry. They totally understood the need to reach young people and even the concept that reaching into schools was possibly the best way of doing this. But the two things that puzzled them about my revelation were that I would place different team members in different churches and that I would make the course free.

REVELATION || YOUR STORY

Now the first part of this test can seem deceiving. People do believe in you. They will come around you. They will even encourage you. But those encouragements will come with warnings.

Do you remember the story of Job's comforters? The ancient writer[29] tells us the story of a man who loved God but was subject to the trial that followed an invisible conversation.[30] The conversation was between God and Satan. In it, God boasts about Job's love for Him, but Satan accuses Job of only loving God because He has treated him so well. To prove the accusation false, God allows Satan to put Job through a living hell. Then, just when it appears that things could not get any worse, Job's friends appear on the scene.

Job's friends take one look at the pitiful sight that was their long-standing companion and immediately make a judgment: he was obviously suffering because of some deep dark secret in his life. This surely had to be the problem; after all, in Old Testament Judaism, black was black and white was white. Bad things would happen to bad people, and good things would happen to good people. That was God's way.[31]

I want you to imagine this from Job's perspective. Job never knew why such terrible things happened to him. In fact, as far as we know, he never found out. The even greater problem was that his friends never knew either.

I think Job's friends get a bit of bad press here. The problem was not simply that they were wrong to judge Job; it was that they had not seen or heard the invisible conversation. Therefore their advice was only aimed at Job, and they had nothing to give him that would help in the bigger picture.

A pioneer keeps going when their friends are more concerned about *them* than *it*.

The second part, then, simply put...

People will resource *you*, but they will not resource *it*.

I found at this stage that people, out of sheer love and concern for me, would happily finance me personally or support me in whatever way they could. The problem with this was that I could not *grow* the vision based on resources I received. I could simply survive.

A third part, then, simply put...

Friends resource *you*, but pioneers resource *it*.

I want to be really honest with you here. If you have a vision, it is going to cost you. You may have to personally sponsor the vision in its initial stages. Lynn and I paid for the first two years of Pais.

I met a friend of mine, Kevin Pimblott, at a motorway service station in the middle of the UK. Kevin was another person God used to empower me at a certain stage of my life. He had many contacts throughout the country, and I was trying to recruit my first few team members. I spent about an hour sharing my idea with him, and he agreed to promote the opportunity wherever he went.

As we were wrapping up, he looked a bit puzzled and asked, "Is that it? Is that all you wanted to know?"

"Yes," I replied.

"But don't you want to know about the money?" he inquired.

He went on to explain that the 46th richest man in Britain had given him scholarship money to subsidize low income youth workers. The conditions were simply that the money would go towards monthly bills and maybe a vacation in the summer. At that point, I was earning around £50[32] a week which was all that my small church could afford to give me. I took that scholarship money, and after several conversations with Kevin where I asked, pleaded, and tried to charm him, it was agreed I could use the money to set up Pais.

So for two years, Lynn and I spent the money that was given to *us*, on *it*.

I am certainly not the only pioneer to have done this. Jamie Oliver, the pioneer chef, is another example. In order to fund his Fifteen Foundation which sponsors disadvantaged young adults and trains them in the restaurant trade, he put up his own house as collateral...without telling his wife.

But let me encourage you: although at this early stage of pioneering, you will need to fund the vision, later others will give far more to *it* than you ever could.

I once heard the true story of a little girl who was sobbing distraughtly having been turned away from a crowded Sunday school. The pastor, looking at her unkempt appearance, guessed the reason for her rejection and personally found a place for her in the class. That night as the little girl meditated on the pastor's great kindness, she lay awake thinking of all the children who had no place to worship Jesus.

Two years later, the little girl's body was found lifeless in a poor apartment block, and her parents called the kindhearted pastor to organize the final arrangements. A ragged purse was found as her body was moved. Inside the purse were 57 cents and a note reading, *"This is to help build the church bigger so more children can go."*

The pastor read the note through teary eyes and was so inspired, he presented it to his congregation the following Sunday. With the tale of her unselfish love, he challenged the congregation to raise the needed funds to construct a larger building. A newspaper picked up the story and published it, which was read by a realtor who hastily offered a large sum of money. Church members donated generously. Within five years, $250,000 was raised, a huge amount at that time.

One child's sacrificial savings resulted in the Temple Baptist Church (seating 3,300), Temple University, the Good Samaritan Hospital, and a large Sunday school building.[33]

Pioneers must be willing to sacrifice for the greater good of others.

roots

An alternative definition of a pioneer is *a plant or animal capable of establishing itself in a bare, barren, or open area and initiating an ecological cycle.*[34] The key word here might be *itself.*

Nobody ever asked me to start the Pais Project. Nobody hired me to do it. Nobody paid me to do it. Nobody even suggested it. For seventeen years until just recently, Pais has been my hobby. During this time, I worked for three churches and in each case was paid for a position within the church. All three of those churches released me in my vision to differing degrees. The first encouraged, the second allowed, the third supported me for the primary purpose of its impact within that church. The drive, however, to push Pais beyond into other cities and nations was not something external but internal. It comes from that seed planted by God, and it needs to take root.

Pioneers tend to be seen as radicals. When people think of radicals, they usually think of crazy maverick extremists; however, the word actually means *growing from the root or from a stem that does not rise above the ground*.[35] In fact, what truly *is* radical about pioneers is a going back to the basics. Pioneers are people who are seeking to return to origins: the original meaning, the original intention, and the original concept.

Most get caught up in programs and systems. They can no longer see the wood for the trees. But pioneers are often lonely because they spend their time digging under the surface for an authentic meaning, an authentic way of achieving what they believe.

What marks the path of a pioneer? The path is not about programs or schedules. It is an unconventional path paved through passion and vision. It is something pioneers see. It is something they feel. It is something they hear. Often it is about getting back to the roots.

questions for the pioneer

1. What is your *it*?

2. Are people displaying a belief in you but not *it*? If so, how are they doing this?

3. Although you may not be able to change this right now, what can you do right now to help these people that may pay off later?

STAGE TWO ✧ REVOLUTION

STAGE TWO

REVOLUTION | MY STORY

abyss

Pais began to grow, but the questions never went away.

During the first year, the little team that I formed fulfilled the vision I had hoped for. Every one of the five churches saw young people come directly from the schools work into the church youth groups.

When I was working on my own, the only youth ministry that had really grown was the one where Joe the pastor came with me. He simply sat in the lunch-time club, and as I presented the teaching, he would just build relationships. Reflecting on that time, he wrote:

> *I remember that before you had a car, sometimes you walked the four miles to the school, and from that lunch time club, the church in Middleton had a youth group that grew from 4 to 20+ of young people loving and serving God and many more that came to the [Manchester] church youth group.*[36]

Now that I had a team of five, the growth multiplied. Rather than having to walk to schools or get a bus, I stepped out in faith and bought a small yellow car. More and more churches heard about the benefit of the team, and more and more schools were opening their doors.

For me, Pais was not really about a program or even the quality of the ministry we did in schools (although that was important). What was primarily important to me was *who* we put into the schools.

Pais is not so much about a new kind of *program*. It's about a new kind of *person*.

While others were caught up with networking and glossy materials, I made the hard decision to build Pais from a grass roots level. This decision would limit growth but aid *authenticity*.

The DNA of that first team was very important, and so I decided that if we were to plant a new team, it would be always be led by someone who had been on

Pais for at least one year. This has become a distinctive of Pais. Rather than investing heavily in promotion, we invest heavily in people.

Joe was the first person to ask for a Pais apprentice. His initial requirements were a male, twenty-one years old or over, with a year's experience as an intern somewhere else. I managed to recruit someone who fit the bill, but Joe decided that he did not fit the church. Eventually they accepted Lisa, an eighteen-year-old high school graduate with no experience and anatomically opposite of the required gender.

Lisa stayed a second year as a team leader. The area which the first team covered was split in two, and she and Gary became the team leaders. We suddenly doubled the young people we could reach and the churches we could impact.

Towards the end of her second year, Lisa began to think of home—her school, her teachers, and the young people of the West Midlands. An idea occurred to us: We should put Pais in her hometown.

By now a number of things made Pais distinctive. It was free. It required second year apprentices to plant new teams. And by putting apprentices in different churches, it was bringing denominations together for one purpose.

A good friend of mine told me that Pais would only work in Manchester because of my relationships there. When I proposed planting it in another part of the country, he listed several reasons why it could not work. However, after a couple of visits to the area, a group of churches agreed to work together, and the Pais team was planted.

Then came another question.

One day I was reading the story of Jesus after His resurrection. His friends had fished all night without catching anything. He approached them, and the following conversation ensued:

> When he had finished speaking, he said to Simon, 'Put out into deep water, and let down the nets for a catch.'

> Simon answered, 'Master, we've worked hard all night and haven't caught anything. But because you say so, I will let down the nets.'
>
> When they had done so, they caught such a large number of fish that their nets began to break. So they signaled their partners in the other boat to come and help them, and they came and filled both boats so full that they began to sink.[37]

A question suddenly popped into my mind. "Paul, if you were one of the disciples and you knew the week beforehand what was going to happen, what would you do?"

Think about that. What would your answer be?

My answer was, "I would spend the entire week building a bigger net."

If, as my translation implied, the disciples caught as many fish as the net could hold, then surely building a bigger net meant catching more fish. It was just common sense. And then I heard one more thing—not so much a question, more a command:

"Go do it then."

Of Jesus' first twelve disciples, five were fishermen. We presume that this was a common vocation among the Jews, but it was not. By nature, Jews were desert nomads. They were afraid of large expanses of water which they called the *abyss*. Places like the Sea of Galilee were looked upon with great suspicion and were believed to abound with evil and chaotic spirits. Few Jews dared to sail across open water, instead remaining close to the shore.

Why did Jesus choose to include five fishermen out of only twelve disciples? It would be like Jesus looking around any large city in America and instead of choosing twelve individuals from twelve different vocations, choosing five oil riggers or five firemen. Jesus' choice of five fishermen was entirely intentional.

Jesus intentionally chose men who dared to live their lives on the edge of the *abyss*, unafraid of both the physical and spiritual danger it presented. They were fishermen who went beyond, and they would go further than their peers. They lived on the edge of the abyss and entered into it.[38]

The five fishermen were people of the 'extra mile' and, like them, my extra mile would be a calling to go beyond the usual.

That conversation has stayed in my mind since the beginning of Pais. I was to build a bigger net. One day Jesus will turn up in our schools and the response will be huge.

But we will only be able to catch as many as the net we have can hold.

But how do you weave a net?

pie

I realized that Pais was going to be just one piece of the pie. There were some organizations that did pretty much everything—conferences, concerts, detached work, but I knew that Pais should never become independent. It was to become *interdependent*.

I soon discovered, however, that not everyone thinks that way.

A great example of this was found in a high school very close to where I lived. In one particular year, this school had the highest absentee rate of any school in England: 42% absent on a typical day. The students were described by one teacher as "totally visionless". Yet we had a major impact in this school, partly due to the fact we partnered with two other organizations. One was the World Wide Message Tribe, led by a friend of mine, Andy Hawthorne. They did phenomenal one-week concerts with a mission on the Friday night. Another group was a smaller Youth for Christ team. They partnered with us on some lessons, and Pais ran a weekly lunchtime club.

It seems to me that the more involved you get with something and the more you find the answer to one question, the more other questions present themselves. As we began making an impact in the school and saw young people slowly filtering into the churches, a new challenge lay ahead...

Some of the churches' youth groups were simply not ready for them.

One of the ways I had been allowed to minister in schools in the first place was by making the decision not to represent a specific church. The local North Manchester Fraternal of Ministers had allowed me to represent them as an entire group, so I was able to print business cards showing I represented many denominations. The Fraternal itself had other benefits. It was a place I could give updates, ask for advice, share needs, and find resources. Local ministers relied on the Fraternal to network, share stories, and ask the 'What would you do if you were in my situation?' kind of questions.

But what about the youth leaders? Few of them were full time, and of those that were, many worked on Pais as well.

Once Pais had established four teams in Manchester, we set up Youth Link. Each month, leaders would come together on a Thursday night. The format was simple: a brief time of worship, a thirty-minute teaching session, a fifteen-minute networking and announcement break, a second teaching session, and a ministry time. Anything that crossed denominational lines and brought unity with a purpose, God seemed to bless. Our numbers grew, and some months we would get around sixty attendees—a mixture of youth pastors, volunteer youth leaders, and Pais apprentices. Eventually, the denomination of which I was a member, adopted Youth Link, catalyzing it into a national program. For a couple of years, over two hundred youth workers met in various towns and cities on a monthly basis. Pais wrote the curriculum, and participants received a certificate at the end of each year.

God blesses unity, but unity is not always a sign of God's blessing.

Sometimes we can be united around unholy things—apathy, a sense of duty, or something else. Youth Link grew because it had a purpose beyond meetings and fellowship. To communicate this, occasionally we held bigger events which included young people from the local schools. We called these events 'Party with a Purpose'.

When the big purpose is lost, unity is pointless. When the big picture is lost, disunity is prevalent.

While Pais was still mainly regional, working in and around Manchester, Youth Link was a high point for me. What had started with Pais—the teaching, principles, and philosophy—was not limited to Pais, but was being reproduced. Young Christian leaders were coming together. New paths and inroads were opened. Missionaries were being made.

But it was not simply other Christians that opened the way...

faiths

Perhaps my greatest advocate in the early days was a Personal, Social, and Health Education teacher. In a three-minute speaking opportunity in the North Manchester school where she taught, I was to address a large assembly of young people where statistically less than 1% went to church and even less knew anything about the Bible. The subject was *The Day of Pentecost*. The following conditions were spelled out for me: no gimmicks, no visuals, and no humor. I had learned that no matter what you were given to do, give it your all. As I practiced this principle, new doors opened and new opportunities arose. So, there in the assembly, I tried to explain the birth of the church, the power of God, and one of the oddest miracles of all time...all in three minutes. In my opinion, the assembly was as flat as a pancake, but the PSE teacher came up to speak to me afterward. Although I had previously contacted her with no response, after hearing the talk, she opened her classroom to me.

She was a Jew.

The first teacher who really opened up to Pais was not a Christian but someone of another faith.

I love atheists. The teachers with no religious affiliation were quite often the best to work with. They had few hang ups, and their general opinion of me was that I was friendly, enthusiastic, and totally harmless. On one occasion in the last twenty years, a group of Muslims caused me problems. But that only lasted for six months, and then they opened their doors. The biggest problem usually came from the Christians.

My first hint of this was when I helped Andy promote *Message 88* in North Manchester. I had few connections at the time, so I cold-called churches that I thought might be interested in local outreach concerts to share the gospel with street kids. As I read through the Yellow Pages, my heart jumped when I saw one church's name: St. John the Evangelist. I called the minister, excited about the potential relationship with a kindred spirit. He asked me what the benefit of having the band would be, and what the purpose was.

I replied, "Evangelism!" with a smile in my voice. His answer will be indelibly etched into my mind:

"Evangelism...we're not really interested in that kind of thing here."

A pioneer's relationship with Christians will often be one of extremes. On one hand I experienced incredible Kingdom-mindedness. The word 'Kingdom-minded' in this sense refers to someone who thought bigger than their own church and put God's bigger purposes first. Earlier I briefly mentioned my pastor, Harry Letson, whom I see as one of the best examples of Kingdom-mindedness.

Harry employed me on £50 a week ($75). Not a lot of money, but I suspected a dip into his personal wage had made this happen. Not long after I began to help my church with its youth and community work, Harry received a call for help from a local church. They had just held a one-week Bible club, and now many more young people were coming to the church but had no youth minister to shepherd them. Despite the needs of our own youth ministry at that time, Harry released me for an entire year to help the church (a different denomination) by serving as their youth pastor. All the while, he still paid my salary.

At the other extreme was when I was working in a particular school and a new youth organization moved into the area. We met and prayed together, and they suggested that two are better than one. Of course they were quite right, so I invited them to come and connect with the teacher. Together we planned and prepared a series of lessons on the resurrection of Jesus that we presented to several grades. Three or four weeks later, a young person from our church asked me, "Why weren't you in the school today?" It turned out that the group had then approached the school separately, organized a new series, but had not included me. When I asked them why they had done this, they replied they did not want to confuse the school with too many Christian organizations approaching them.

"We don't want to confuse people."

It has become a line I have heard several times since.

Chatting with the teacher, however, revealed that her principal had said to her, "The more the merrier—in fact it helps having more than one organization because it guards us against the accusation of allowing proselytization for one particular church or group."

grass

The world is a desperate place.

If you've watched any TV, you've probably seen some terrible news about an awful tragedy, injustice, or atrocious act. For most of my life these stories happened overseas in some distant land. This misconception changed, however, when one evening a reporter began to tell the story of Susan. Susan was a fifteen-year-old girl who had been kidnapped, held hostage, and tortured for an entire week. At the end of the week, her torturers took her a few miles away, removed her teeth to prevent identification through dental records, poured gasoline on her, and burned her to death. Before she died, she managed to crawl to a road where a passer-by spotted her and contacted an ambulance. On her death bed, Susan told the police what had happened to her and who had done this terrible thing. Then the news program put up the pictures of the killers who, inspired by the film *Child's Play*, had abused and murdered her. As Lynn and I sat there in front of the TV, our mouths dropped opened...

We knew them.

THE LINE AND THE DOT ⋅⋅⋅ STAGE TWO

Our lovely, gentle, and kind next-door neighbor was their grandfather. The news reporters then proceeded to show pictures of a large three-foot wooden spoon that Susan had been tied to. Lynn could not believe it—she had often gone to the killers' house to cut their hair (in her job as a mobile hairdresser) and she moved the spoon off the wall of their small Moston house kitchen in order to get around.

As shocking as this was to her, what came next made me sick to my stomach.

As it concluded, the report showed the house where this young girl had been held captive: It was a stone's throw from ours. During that week I had walked past that house four times each day. To work in the morning, back for lunch, back to work in the afternoon, and at the end of the day to return home. Twenty times that week I walked past that house. Where was I going?

To my church office.

Twenty times I had passed this place of desperation, totally unaware of what was going on behind its red brick wall.

Where did Susan go to school?

To the one we did not want to..."confuse".

In my journey as a pioneer, I have seen too many Christian brothers and sisters who have lost sight of why they were called.

We are the ones confused.

When bull elephants fight, the grass always loses. - An African proverb.

questions for the pioneer

1. Who would you say is for you and who would you say is against you?

2. Do you feel you own the vision or it is simply being entrusted to you? What is the difference?

3. Does the end justify the means? Could it be that your victories carry the seeds of future defeats?

STAGE TWO

REVOLUTION | OUR STORY

revolution

Most of us have some kind of vision, some kind of idea, a yearning to go farther, to break free, to create. And yet invisible barriers seem to fence us in. What are these hidden fences?

The second stage all pioneers go through is the stage of revolution.

Pioneers break the system. Or so it seems.

> *At that time Jesus went through the grainfields on the Sabbath. His disciples were hungry and began to pick some heads of grain and eat them. When the Pharisees saw this, they said to him, "Look! Your disciples are doing what is unlawful on the Sabbath."*[39]

At the revelation stage, people around the pioneer simply think he or she is a dreamer, but at this stage the seed of a dream begins to sprout and show itself on the surface. To others' amazement, *it* seems to be working. The pioneer's vision appears to have unlimited potential to break the system and reach beyond what is humanly conceivable. In reality, dreams, visions, and yearnings can only be restrained by God Himself or by the limitations of the pioneer.

Let me put it this way. If the line represents the traditional and common way of living our lives, barriers at either end of the line stop us from going beyond ourselves.

These 'hidden hedges' must be broken. As they break, we will go further than we have ever gone before. The line will become a distant memory. We will think back to a day when line-dwelling was all we knew but move forward into a future where the line has become no more than a dot to us.

Like most members of the Gibbs family, I am not a great sportsman, but like most Gibbs, I swim really well. My dad is a great swimmer; my grandmother swam for the City of London competitively. Most families remember key moments in their child's upbringing: the first word, the first steps, and the first tooth. Our family has an addition to that: the first pool-length swim.

One day, when my eldest son Joel was seven years old, I took the family swimming at the local pool. I'll never forget when Joel came up to me and said, "Dad, I think this is the day I can do it. I think I can go farther than I have before." I was excited—he wanted to swim the length of the pool! I knew this was going to be one of those defining bonding experiences.

I encouraged him, "We can do it, son; we can do it together!"

"But, Dad," he said, "I'm nervous. I'm really, really nervous. I want to do it, but I need some encouragement."

"Like what? What can I do to help you?"

"Maybe if I make it, I can get some kind of reward."

"Like what?" I asked him.

"A Playstation," he replied.

After brief negotiations and the promise of a secondhand Playstation 1, we dove into the pool together.

Joel started strong. I was proud.

Then he began to struggle. I was concerned.

"It's hard, Dad! It's hard!"

"Come on, son, you can do it!" I replied.

"Is there anything else, Dad? Anything else I could have if I make it?"

We treaded water together...fifteen meters to go. "What about a game to go with the console?"

Inspired by these rewards Joel, my hero, pushed through the pain barrier and his fear and made it to the end of the pool. I cheered and hugged him. Grabbing his hand, I ran to his mother, excited about telling her what we had accomplished together. I gushed to Lynn of his wonderful feat, his courage, his determination to go beyond his limits. I will always remember her face as she looked me deep in the eyes and said...

"What are you talking about? He's been able to swim a length for six months."

She went on to explain that half a year ago he swam a length and received his official certificate, and since then, had done it on a regular basis. I looked down and there was my son, a big smile on his face, the promise of a Playstation and game firmly secured, his face the epitome of what the English call..."cheeky".

Pioneers must have more than simply the appearance of going farther than they have before.

But what pins us back? What keeps us trapped within that comfort zone?

hedge #1 - word

There is a hint. There is a clue. There is an intimation.

God is a pioneer. He tells us His story, but something tells us He's not telling us everything.

For instance:

> *In the beginning God created the heavens and the earth.*[40]

Simple...or is it?

During the 11th century, a Jewish rabbi from France named Rashi discovered a bit of information, a subtle suggestion, which throughout the ages has created much opportunity for discourse and debate among those who study the Torah. What the rabbi noticed was an oddity in the structure of the first word of the first verse in the first chapter of the Bible: "In the beginning."

If the intended meaning of the word for *in the beginning* was *at first* or *in-beginning*, the obvious Hebrew word used would have been *b'rishonah*.

Instead God tells us His story using the word *b'reishit*, which actually means *in-beginning-of*.

In-beginning-of God created the heavens and the earth.

This leads to the obvious question: "In the beginning of *what?*"

Exactly *what* was God in the beginning of when He created the heavens and the earth?

A game of Monopoly?

Wallpapering the living room?

Although there are many nuances, eventually the majority of rabbis came to the conclusion that He was in-beginning-of...*going beyond Himself.*

It seems if we are to believe these Judaic scholars and their interpretation, then God created because He went *beyond* Himself. But how can God possibly go beyond Himself? God is everywhere! A further understanding leads us to believe that God created an opportunity to pour out His love.

God is love.[41]

God is a *pioneer* of love.

God's love is so huge that He created something that did not exist; He created opportunity. God's love is very different from any other love—it is not reactionary and it is not conditional on how He feels. In the Greek, several words explain different types of love. The three most common are *eros*, *philo*, and *agape*.

Eros is a sensual love. It says, "I love you because you make me feel good."

Philo is a brotherly love. It says, "I love you because together we are good."

Agape is God's love. It essentially says, "I love you because I am love."

If we have God's *agape* love, we will create opportunities to show it. God is a God of expansion. Both the Father and Son created a way that did not exist. Pioneers are those who have that same spirit within them. We create, not because people make us feel a certain way, nor because it is necessarily good for us. Our driving force is love.

starfish

There is a famous story that preachers love to tell. It is intended to motivate people to make a difference.

An adult wanders onto a beach and sees a boy trying to rescue thousands of starfish stranded on the sand. The boy slowly and meticulously picks up the starfish and throws it back into the sea, and then another one, and then another one. The adult asks the boy, "Why are you bothering? There are millions of starfish on the beach; you'll never be able to make a difference." The little boy replied as he picked up yet another starfish and threw it back into the sea, "Yes, but I can make a difference to this one."

I hate the starfish story.

I am with the adult... *Buy yourself a tractor!*

There are thousands of starfish on the beach, and there are millions dying without Christ. I understand the point of the starfish story. It is to encourage us when we feel overwhelmed by the need that we can still make a difference to some. But my problem is this: I think the starfish story sums up the attitude of so many because it essentially says, "At least I'm doing my bit." It is reactionary. It relieves us from guilt. It immunizes us from the heartache that perhaps we should feel.

Jesus was a rabbi. The word rabbi means *master* or *great one*, deriving from the word *rav* meaning *many*, *numerous*, and *great*. Rabbis were to make *many* disciples. The Mishnah, a compilation of the oral law, had instructions for rabbis. It said this:

> Be deliberate in judgment, make many disciples, and put a fence around the Torah.[42]

The ancient rabbi Hillel was said to have waited outside the city gates each morning, urging people not to go to work that day but spend it learning the Torah from him. His grandson, Gamaliel the elder, was said to have had at least 1000 disciples. Paul the apostle, a Pharisee and one of Gamaliel's students, traveled the known world to make disciples. We think of Jesus having twelve disciples, but of course He had many more than that. He had the seventy He sent out. We know of 120 disciples from Galilee alone who remained in Jerusalem after His crucifixion. Of the multitudes that honored Him as He entered Jerusalem, many would have been disciples He made while travelling throughout the towns and villages.

Pioneers are those who go beyond themselves. My going beyond was reaching into schools. It is said that 83% of people who become Christians do so between the age of four and fourteen.[43] To me, the concept that our churches would put so little of their budget into young people seemed senseless. The little that they did spend was usually on those already in the church. Reaching into schools where the vast majority of young people are—regardless of their background, religion, or ethnicity—was common sense. But a system had to be broken.

There is a hidden hedge. It is a missing word.

Too many are waiting to be given this word. It might be the word *go*. It may be the word *salary*. It could be the word *praise*. Many are bound—limited by the fact that they are waiting to be told to do something. But true pioneers are those who go beyond what they are told to do. They go further than a word they are given.

The most significant thing you will do for God is the one thing that no one tells you to do.

hedge # 2 - attitude

If the first hidden hedge was an invisible word, then the second one is an invisible attitude.

There's an attitude of the Pioneer Jesus that has been lost over time.

> *"Teacher," said John, "we saw a man driving out demons in your name and we told him to stop, because he was not one of us."*

> *"Do not stop him,"* Jesus said. *"No one who does a miracle in my name can in the next moment say anything bad about me, for whoever is not against us is for us."*[44]

Four times the gospels record Jesus using this kind of phrase. Twice in the negative: *"If they are not for me they are against me."* And twice in the positive: *"If they are not against you, they are for you."*

I have heard the negative preached and spoken many times. But I cannot remember the second statement, recorded just as often, ever being taught. If Hebrews is right when it says we need to look to Jesus as a role model of pioneering, then this statement has to have huge significance in our thinking. There are two mistakes we tend to make. First, we approach the world as being against us unless it is for us; and second, what we really mean by *for us* is *part of us*.

The biggest obstacles I have faced are Christians who believe that greater is he who is in the world than He who is in them.

A supportive Christian teacher once gave me an opportunity to start a lunch-time club in an all-boys school. Around thirty young boys attended each week, many who were of the Islamic faith. At one point, the teacher said to me, "Paul, if the parents of these boys find out, there could be trouble ahead." She decided to change the time of the club to make it more difficult, therefore filtering out the least committed; we would have it after-school. It worked. The numbers dropped considerably. Just over half came. But every single one of them was Muslim. A week later, we shut the club down completely.

Pioneers must avoid the pressure of polarization.

Many years ago in Britain, communities gathered together in two places. One of the places was called a public house. Like a typical house but much bigger, they catered to large gatherings and contained game rooms, kitchens, and lounges. The community met at a public house for fun, relaxation, and laughter. The other place was the church. The community gathered here to learn together, worship together, and serve together.

One day the owners of the public houses decided that if people were not for them, then they were against them. They told the community, "It's us or them. Choose." And there was a split. Two groups of people began to develop, and as time went by, one group became larger, but the influence of both groups slowly diminished.

What is wrong with this story?

It is not entirely true.

It was not the owners of the public houses but the 'owners' of the churches that created the division. This story, although oversimplified, shows how this hidden hedge can limit us from going beyond ourselves.

An American parallel may possibly be the separation of Church and State. When I came to America, I presumed that this was something the State had implemented. I was surprised to find out, however, that this belief system was created to calm the fears of the nation's Christian founders. The first record of this phrase being used was by Thomas Jefferson who wrote to a Baptist church:

> *Believing with you that religion is a matter which lies solely between Man and his God, that he owes account to none other for his faith or his worship, that the legitimate powers of government reach actions only, and not opinions, I contemplate with sovereign reverence that act of the whole American people which declared that their legislature should "make no law respecting an establishment of religion, or prohibiting the free exercise thereof," thus building a wall of separation between Church and State.*[45]

I fully understand that this is a deeply complex issue, but I just want to point out that it was this imagining of a worst-case scenario that led to the situation which many Christians now think is insurmountable.

The worst use of imagination is to imagine the worst.

hacienda

This week my eldest son was sent to the principal's office for using a 'fake' British accent while in class. As he was about to leave the room, the substitute teacher dismissed him with the words, "You're doing a good job, but please stop it!" It took several of Joel's classmates to convince her that he was in fact English.

Jesus created a revolution partly because He got to know people well enough not to pre-judge them. His revolution was one of relationship. When so many religious leaders labeled entire groups of people, Jesus did not. There was something about His attitude of entering into the world that was different. Those with the spirit of a pioneer must have a similar attitude. Understand it will cause a similar revolution.

The disciples had an attitude of pre-judging and so:

> *Jesus told them another parable: "The Kingdom of Heaven is like a man who sowed good seed in his field. But while everyone was sleeping, his enemy came and sowed weeds among the wheat, and went away. When the wheat sprouted and formed heads, then the weeds also appeared.*
>
> *"The owner's servants came to him and said, 'Sir, didn't you sow good seed in your field? Where then did the weeds come from?'*
>
> *'An enemy did this,' he replied.*
>
> *"The servants asked him, 'Do you want us to go and pull them up?'*
>
> *'No,' he answered, 'because while you are pulling the weeds, you may root up the wheat with them.'"*[46]

The word *weeds* used here is misleading. The Hebrew transliteration Jesus would have actually spoken is *zonin*.[47] Zonin is a degenerate form of wheat. It looks like wheat, but it does not reproduce what is required. The key here is that the difference is only visible to the eye when the head appears. So what is Jesus saying? He is saying that we need to approach the world with an attitude that it is *for us*, that is ready to harvest unless they have had their *final opportunity*.[48]

REVOLUTION || OUR STORY

Of course, sometimes it may be wrong to set foot in certain places.

At the age of eighteen, four years after I'd become a follower of Jesus, I turned my back on Him, and one of the first things I did was join what became an infamous nightclub in Manchester. I was one of the first members of the Hacienda, and it was full of sinners like me. Now if I say it was wrong for me to go there because there was sin in that place, I would be condemning Jesus; Jesus went to the homes of sinners, and where sinners gather, there is going to be sin. Yet it was wrong for me to go there.

Why?

I was wrong for going there, not because of the wrong inside the nightclub but because of the wrong inside of me looking to connect with the wrong inside of the nightclub.

Only God knows why we set foot in certain places and how pure our motives are for doing so. However, it is also true that only God knows why we do *not* set foot in certain places and how pure our motives are for *not* doing so.

hedge # 3 - practice

The third part of Jesus' revolution was the issue He had with the religious culture of the day. These cultural issues and the paradigm that they established still affect you and me today in our Christian and even post-Christian environments.

When Moses went up Mount Sinai and met with God, he received the Law. In our western minds when we think of the Law we think of something that is negative and harsh, but in the Jewish mindset, Torah means *Way*. It was not simply a set of rules and regulations; it was instruction on how to live, guidelines that would bind the community together. It was said that Moses received the written law but also he received the oral law. The Pharisees believed that this oral law was just as authoritative as the written law. The Sadducees did not. The oral law was an explanation that was built over time and added to, establishing guidelines on how to live according to the written law. In Jesus' time, the Sadducees were responsible for the Temple and many of its ceremonies, while the Pharisees were seen as the experts in these religious regulations. It gave them power; it gave them control.

The religious culture at this time believed in 'light' and 'heavy' commandments. The teachers of the Law instructed people that they should obey even the smallest commands for two important reasons. The first, they said, was that no one really knew how seriously God took even the light commands. The second was that if you broke a light command, you would eventually break a heavy command. Both reasons were intended to keep Israel from breaking God's laws. In doing so, the people would avoid punishment and gain a reward.

Now if you remember, this oral law had a three part command to rabbis:

> *Be deliberate in judgment, make many disciples, and put a fence around the Torah.*[49]

When you see the phrase *put a fence around the Torah*, what does that mean to you? Does it conjure up the idea of protecting the Torah? The problem is that the Torah does not need protecting. God's Word does not need human defense. The phrase meant something very different. It refers to a particular religious practice held by the Pharisees. To avoid sin, the religious leaders would put a 'fence' around the Torah. The rabbis would bind and loosen their disciples, meaning they would interpret the Law and give practical commands to their followers. They would bind, or in other words forbid, their disciples to do certain things based on their interpretation of the Law. They would also loosen, or permit, their disciples to do certain things. Essentially this is how it worked: if something was seen as a sin, they would bind their disciples by putting a buffer between the sin and what their followers were allowed to do. They would restrict them from even going anywhere near it by creating a new law. They would therefore put a fence around God's commandment.

One example of this is found in their interpretation of the Torah scripture:

> *Remember the Sabbath day by keeping it holy.*[50]

By the time Jesus was walking around Jerusalem, reams and reams of additional oral laws (or fences) existed. In fact, years after Jesus' death and resurrection, there were thirty-nine categories of things a Jew could not do on the Sabbath. We are not talking about thirty-nine restrictions; we are talking about thirty-nine *categories* of restrictions.

Their premise was essentially this: on a scale of one to ten, ten representing the sin that God forbid them from, they would create a fence by making a new law which said that no one should go as far as number nine. In their world, if they stopped people from going as far as number nine, then they could avoid the possibility of someone committing a number ten.

I-30

Jesus as a pioneer, although understanding the importance of light and heavy commands, seemed to have four major issues with these fences.

The first issue is that we rely on the system rather than the Spirit.

People love systems. But the problem with a system is that, as Christians, we often do just what the system tells us to. We *react* to the system rather than *pro-act* because of the Spirit's moving. We only go as far as the system tells us we have to go. Therefore, the system can eventually bind us from creating opportunity and going beyond. These systems, although not innately bad, create a line on which we live, limited at both ends by man-made hedges. The Spirit wants to lead us beyond these limitations. These fences should be our servants; we should not become their slaves. If we live by the Spirit, the Spirit will catapult us to a place where the line has become a dot to us.

> *Going on from that place, he went into their synagogue, and a man with a shriveled hand was there. Looking for a reason to accuse Jesus, they asked him, "Is it lawful to heal on the Sabbath?"*
>
> *He said to them, "If any of you has a sheep and it falls into a pit on the Sabbath, will you not take hold of it and lift it out? How much more valuable is a man than a sheep! Therefore it is lawful to do good on the Sabbath."*

> *Then he said to the man, "Stretch out your hand." So he stretched it out and it was completely restored, just as sound as the other. But the Pharisees went out and plotted how they might kill Jesus.*[51]

Jesus put *humanity* before *hedges*.

Not far from my house is Interstate 30. It has a speed limit of sixty miles per hour. For argument's sake, let's just say this represents God's law. If I were to go above sixty miles per hour, I would be breaking God's law. Now if the Pharisees were alive today they might say: in order that you do not break God's law, we will create a fence. The fence will keep you from going beyond fifty-five miles per hour so that you cannot *possibly* break God's law of sixty miles per hour.

This was not a problem to the Pharisees who believed God would rescue His people when they cleaned up their act. This was pure common sense. One day, however, a young pregnant wife goes into labor. Her husband helps her into the car and they set off on I-30 to get her to the hospital as soon as possible. He goes as fast as God's law allows him—sixty miles per hour. The Pharisees stop and condemn him. "How dare you break the law!" they say.

Whose law are they breaking though? Their law, not God's. These teachers of the Law were putting the *system* before the *Spirit*. Jesus referred to these 'fences' as: *"the traditions of men."*[52]

Jesus would pioneer a new radical path. It would revolutionize society. It would remind people of the heart of God's commands. But to do this, He would call these practices, these traditions of men, simply *"a fine way of setting aside the commands of God!"*[53]

One way to know if a vision is truly from God is if it puts *humanity* before *hedges*. Revolutionary vision will create a path from God to people and people to God without the objective of control, power, or status.

As one author lamented:

> *When I was growing up in Belfast, I attended a church so exclusive that we doubted the salvation of just about anyone outside our own ranks.*

> *We fought over the Godhead, water baptism, women wearing hats and keeping the Old Testament food laws. We even sang a chorus in church, "Keep the food laws, they are good laws, praise the Lord, I'm feeling fine since I left off eating swine." You may smile, but that's where we put our energies, while half the world was dying without Christ. Thank God we've grown up since then.*[54]

The second problem Jesus had with this system of fences is that they provide a way in which we are tempted to compare ourselves with each other.

> *To some who were confident of their own righteousness and looked down on everybody else, Jesus told this parable: "Two men went up to the temple to pray, one a Pharisee and the other a tax collector. The Pharisee stood up and prayed about himself: 'God, I thank you that I am not like other men—robbers, evildoers, adulterers—or even like this tax collector. I fast twice a week and give a tenth of all I get.'*
>
> *"But the tax collector stood at a distance. He would not even look up to heaven, but beat his breast and said, 'God, have mercy on me, a sinner.'*
>
> *"I tell you that this man, rather than the other, went home justified before God. For everyone who exalts himself will be humbled, and he who humbles himself will be exalted."*[55]

The desire of the Spirit is to work within us in such a way that we aspire to be like Jesus. He accomplishes this by convicting and challenging us to go beyond the boundaries of our flesh. Fences, however, give us a system that enables us to feel good about ourselves—at least we're better than the person next to us. Rather than feeling desperate for God's righteousness, we become confident *in our own* righteousness. This parable was told by Jesus because He observed many in His audience who were confident they were better than others.

Question: How can you possibly be confident in your own righteousness? The answer is actually simpler than you might imagine.

As an Englishman living in America, and assuming I was reasonably fit, I would be confident in my ability to beat most people in a game of soccer. If the sport were American football, however, my confidence would disappear unless...

...Unless I had the power to make up the rules as I went along. In that case, my opposition would not be allowed to touch me, would not wear protective clothing, and with my new rules, I could kick them.

Why were the Pharisees confident in their own righteousness? Because they made up their own rules as they went along.

A third issue Jesus had is that fences provide a barrier between us and the world.

The world you cannot *enter* is the world you cannot *reach*.

I wonder if the disciples ever hesitated.

Disciples were known to be fanatical in their desire to stick close to their rabbi, so close that they would cover their heads with the dust from his feet. They would go everywhere with him.

I can think of one situation though where Jesus' disciples may have hesitated. Perhaps they were walking down the road one day, sticking close to Jesus as He spoke to passers-by, as He shopped in the market place, as He rested under a palm tree. They walked with Him along the road, but suddenly He turned and walked into the home of a well-known sinner. Did these young men of fifteen and sixteen years old, brought up in a society where religion is everything, pause? Did they stop maybe momentarily at the doorway thinking to themselves, "Is He serious? Does he really want us to go in *there*?"

The Spirit of God is calling pioneers to follow Him in *there*. And going in there will cause a revolution. It will create questions, provoke accusations, or may simply just produce smiles at your naivety and foolishness. It is not a place most people go.

A fourth issue Jesus had is that ultimately fences can create a system between us and God.

> *You shall not take the name of the LORD your God in vain.*[56]

The original interpretation of this written law of God was that you must keep your vow when swearing by God's name. But later, as fences were introduced, it was said that you should not even swear in God's name because a vow never made can never be broken. As time went by, people were bound from saying the name of God lightly, and then by the time Jesus arrived on the scene, to say the name of God at all was forbidden. In Jesus' day the Tetragrammaton, the four Hebrew letters usually transliterated YHWH or JHVH that form a Biblically proper name of God, could only be uttered in the Temple, in the daily blessing, and confession of high priest on the Day of Atonement.

What can we learn about this third hidden hedge? And why is it important for pioneers? Pioneers are people who are simply not bound by man's systems. Jesus was not; He clearly understood their value, but was not bound by them.

Fences should be our servants. And we should take caution never to become their slaves.

new

Why do I say this practice is a hidden hedge? What relevance does this have to us? For those of us who have been Christians for a while, we understand we are part of a new covenant.

For many, these old laws became like a blindfold. They stopped them from seeing possibilities. They hindered the people of God from truly being salt and light in the world.

We may be rid of old laws, but have we simply created a whole new set of replacement laws instead?

Are we walking around with a *new* blindfold?

Somewhere deep inside, we know there are fences in place that are less about God and more about men. Yet what holds us back is when we look around, everybody is penned in the same way. We have ideas of things that we *should* or *could* do, but the reality and the normality of our religious culture makes us think to ourselves, "It must just be me." Jesus came to a community of people that really should have known better. The problem was everybody was doing it.

For a revolution to take place, there needs to be that one person who is willing to break free and create...to think outside the box...to be willing to go where no one has gone before.

To create a revolution, you must not be held back by a hidden word. Instead of waiting for someone to tell you, do it because the Spirit of God has revealed it to you.

To create a revolution, you must not be held back by a hidden attitude. Instead of seeing the world as against you, enter it as though it is for you.

To create a revolution, you must not be held back by a hidden practice. Instead of putting fences first, put humanity before hedges.

REVOLUTION || OUR STORY

questions for the pioneer

1. With Hedge # 1 in mind, what are you waiting for?

2. With Hedge # 2 in mind, who are you waiting for?

3. With Hedge # 3 in mind, what have you put in your way?

STAGE TWO

REVOLUTION | YOUR STORY

threat

The Encarta dictionary defines the word *oxymoron* as 'a phrase in which two words of contradictory meaning are used together for special effect'. Here are a few examples: Act Naturally. Found Missing. Good Grief. Living Dead. Pretty Ugly. Microsoft Works.

Let me just rant here for a moment. From England, I moved to Texas where I was offered the drink 'Iced Tea'.

Iced tea is an oxymoron.

Iced tea is simply not right. Tea is meant to be hot. If God wanted tea to be cold, we would pick leaves in Alaska. We pick tea leaves in India, and India is hot—It is a hint.

Iced tea is just dirty water!

'Iced tea'...yet another example of what goes wrong when man plays God.

The phrase 'A Pioneer' is again an oxymoron, two words that simply do not fit together. It is true that it takes one person to change the world. But, that one person can never do it alone. A pioneer needs to be plural not singular.

For you as a pioneer, one of the most important assets you will ever need is the gift to build a team.

Building a team, however, is not as easy as you may suppose. You might think that simply getting a vision from God is enough. You might think that everyone surely would want to get on board. The fact, however, is that not all martyrs died at the hands of unbelievers. Therefore, to see God's vision fully realized, you will need to pass the test of being seen as a *threat*.

issue

In the first stage of pioneering, which is Revelation, the test you go through is the one of being a loner. People believe in *you* but they do not believe in *it*. Those in authority, the ones who hold the resources and platform you might need, may like your energy and enthusiasm but will potentially be a little patronizing. They do not fully understand your vision or, if they do, they simply do not think it will work or grow.

In the second stage, entitled Revolution, the same people who patronized you may now be surprised to see your idea flourish. Suddenly they take it a little more seriously. Now bear in mind, many will indeed be thrilled about your vision and want to get on board, but this book is intended to provide the full picture of what it means to become a pioneer. Therefore, you must recognize that *some* people, as they take you more seriously, will suddenly realize the implications of your vision to their own situation.

> At that time Jesus went through the grain fields on the Sabbath. His disciples were hungry and began to pick some heads of grain and eat them. When the Pharisees saw this, they said to him, "Look! Your disciples are doing what is unlawful on the Sabbath."
>
> He answered, "Haven't you read what David did when he and his companions were hungry? He entered the house of God, and he and his companions ate the consecrated bread—which was not lawful for them to do, but only for the priests. Or haven't you read in the Law that on the Sabbath the priests in the temple desecrate the day and yet are innocent? I tell you that one greater than the temple is here. If you had known what these words mean, 'I desire mercy, not sacrifice,' you would not have condemned the innocent. For the Son of Man is Lord of the Sabbath."[57]

Remember the fences?

This is a classic case of a group of leaders feeling threatened. The Pharisees' power was based on the fact that the oral law was as authoritative as the written law and they were the best interpreters of this oral law. Here, a number of Jesus' followers appear to break that oral law. Immediately the Pharisees see this Jesus, a rabbi growing in popularity, as a risk to their position. The fact that Jesus' answer is brilliant does not help.

Sometimes the issue is not really the issue.

The Kingdom comes when extra miles are *disclosed* and when evil intentions are *exposed*.

Jesus' ministry was all about revealing hidden things.

> *So do not be afraid of them. There is nothing concealed that will not be disclosed, or hidden that will not be made known.*[58]

Jesus purposely provoked; He said and did things to stir up evil. Where He went, demons were exposed and so were the religion, laws, and systems behind which they hid.

Why would He do this?

So that observers would be presented with the opportunity to make a choice.

Most hedges are hidden. The attitudes, motives, and instinct for self-preservation that limit right living are often camouflaged. Evil lurks like a sniper whose goal is to blend into his surroundings by painting his skin and wearing a disguise to conceal himself. The unveiling of these 'hidden hedges' is essential if people are to see the difference between the kingdom of *self* and the Kingdom of *God*.

Jesus the pioneer had a plan of action…

He provoked.

This forced that which was hidden to be exposed. The camouflage of religion, the disguise of law, the cover-up of *systems* began to fall away as people came out of the shadows to attack Jesus.

The second part of Jesus' plan was to react in a godly way. As He was persecuted, lied about, and beaten, He kept quiet, and eventually those around Him were able to see what they could not see before. Jesus provoked evil into the light. By being good and exposing evil as evil, a contrast became evident for all to see.

If Jesus had provoked evil into the light and then reacted in the same way as His opposition, although He would have been right, most of the onlookers would have simply been confused. What can help people see the contrast between evil and good, and therefore make a choice, is not always the argument, but the *action* and the way in which we bring our argument.

Evil had been exposed, and people could freely reject it. They now saw a clear contrast between good and evil and were presented with the opportunity to walk this new path called the Kingdom of Heaven. Their eyes were opened as they saw this juxtaposition of a pioneer of the Kingdom and the prisoners of self.

As pioneers, we must fix our eyes on Jesus, not simply on what He achieved by pioneering, but on who He is as a pioneer.

mafia

A mistake many pioneers make is that because God has given us a vision, we think we can behave in any manner we desire. God, however, does not bless *vision*, He blesses the *visionary*.

The vision He gives is already pure.

The question for success therefore becomes, "Is the *visionary* pure?"

There are several ways in which the test of threat manifests itself. Likewise, there are several ways in which you as the pioneer must respond in order to keep your heart, motives, and identity intact.

The first manifestation of threat is withdrawal.

Those who have resources but feel threatened, tend to withdraw those resources. In an effort to counteract this potential tendency, Pais puts numerous missionaries in the field for an extremely low cost. Pais does not need vast sums of money, simply because we're all about partnership. What we do need, however, is platform, profile…essentially any chance to recruit. I hit upon a problem.

A unique distinctive of Pais is that our opportunities are free, and food and accommodation are provided. The typical economic model of other apprenticeship programs is that each intern raises not just their own support, but a fee for the organization, usually somewhere between £3000-5000 [around $6000] per year. This covers their training, and a portion of their money goes to the organization through which they serve.

Around the time I founded Pais, several of these programs were in operation. For whatever reason, God compelled me to make Pais apprenticeships free. I did not see the fact that others charged as a negative; I just knew I was not supposed to, and this created a problem.

The best place to promote Pais and to share the story was at events, conferences, and colleges, but many of these places were run by organizations with their own internship programs. Obviously, this made it difficult for them to promote Pais alongside their opportunities—"Why not take up these three opportunities that cost $6000 or this one that is exactly the same, but free."

How does a pioneer respond in this situation? It is often a struggle to keep your attitude right, but as a wise man once said:

> "Guard your heart for it is the wellspring of life."[59]

We do it by responding exactly the opposite way. On countless occasions over the years, great leaders with their own internships have been invited to speak at Pais conferences. Leaders who are far more charismatic, and better speakers than I will ever be, have stood on the Pais platform and shared their vision. I confess that this was often a struggle. Many times I grudgingly invited others, not because they were not great speakers, but because they *were* great speakers.

I had to make sure that I did not join the Mafia.

As my ministry grew, I gradually became a person with resources, authority, and control. A group of schools workers in Manchester met on a regular basis. At one meeting, someone suggested we form a committee that would vet schools work in Manchester. The proposal was that as we were the ones with opportunities in schools, and since we'd worked so hard to create them, we should ensure that the less experienced schools workers could not ruin it for the rest of us. In that meeting, the idea began to be formatted. Green horns would have to come and meet with us, convince us of their material, and allow us to ensure they met our standards. As the conversation went on, the sicker I began to feel. I would not become like the system I had struggled with so much. As the discussion gained momentum, I shared my concerns and ruled myself out.

Stay in the system too long and, if you're not careful, you become part of it. For all our good intentions, we cannot sit on the fence.

topple

The second manifestation of threat is the obstacles *others* see.

> *You see, at just the right time, when we were still powerless, Christ died for the ungodly. Very rarely will anyone die for a righteous man, though for a good man someone might possibly dare to die. But God demonstrates his own love for us in this: While we were still sinners, Christ died for us.*[60]

There seems to be a misconception about visionaries…an incorrect assumption they do not see obstacles. But pioneers are totally aware of the obstacles. In fact, they often see them before anyone else.

What makes a pioneer a pioneer are the revolutionary ways in which they overcome obstacles. They are not blind to the obstacle; on the contrary, they see a way through it.

Jesus was aware of the obstacle of sin. He was not blind to it; He saw a way through it.

When people feel threatened, they have a habit of blowing up any cracks or flaws in the plan. Since Pais was at no cost to the apprentice, many of our members who stayed long term knew they were committing to a lifestyle that would likely have a low income. Before long, we were labeled with having a poverty mindset. I would sometimes even be at a conference where people would jokingly pass me their leftover food and tell me to take it home to my children so they could have something to eat. This can affect people in different ways; we can be tempted to feel hurt, embarrassed, or disappointed. For me it was mainly an overwhelming feeling of frustration. Pais is definitely not a career that will make you financially wealthy… I understood and still understand that. But I do firmly believe that if we seek first the Kingdom of God, He will give us all we need. Even though many of those around me believe the same thing, the economics of Pais became an obstacle that they saw as an insurmountable wall.

One time a CEO, speaking on how to cope with criticism, told the story of an architect who said:

> *"I can take the newest building, built by the finest builders anywhere in the world, and if you give me a camera and the ability to focus various lenses, I can make that building look like it's about to fall down because I will find five or six minor imperfections, focus on them and convince you that the entire structure is about to topple."*[61]

How do you cope with the obstacles others see? Perhaps my best advice would be to try and understand *why* people focus on obstacles. One reason could simply be that they have not yet had the revelation of how to overcome them.

Or, it could be that they *have*.

Many years ago, a survey was taken asking retired people, "What is your biggest regret in life?"[62]

In the top five answers, the most prominent was…

Not taking enough risks.

Why do people feel threatened? Sometimes they feel threatened by the fact that they did not do it themselves.

Remember that others may have seen the possibility but simply decided not to go there because it was 'impossible'. While nobody was doing it, the theory that it was impossible held water. But now here you come. You are potentially going to do what was previously seen as unachievable. If you do it, the excuse they held on to is going to be blown apart.

knife

The third manifestation of threat is personality.

Ultimately, we have to remember the person we are fighting is invisible.

> *For our struggle is not against flesh and blood, but against the rulers, against the authorities, against the powers of this dark world and against the spiritual forces of evil in the heavenly realms.*[63]

The writer of this letter uses this word *against* several times. The original word specifically refers to hand-to-hand battles. Pioneering can get very personal. However, the personality we are really dealing with is a spiritual one.

To react humanly to a spiritual battle is tantamount to bringing a knife to a gun fight.

Although it is not primarily an emotional battle, we engage our emotions before we engage our spirit. Although it is not primarily an intellectual battle, we engage our minds before we engage our spirit.

Do you remember Jesus' statement about turning the other cheek? Although legendary, this statement is often misunderstood.

> *But I tell you, do not resist an evil person. If someone strikes you on the right cheek, turn to him the other also.*[64]

Notice, Jesus purposely mentions the right cheek. He's emphasizing a certain type of cheek-slapping—a back-handed slap to a person's right cheek. This type of blow would result in a minor amount of pain, but was considered particularly insulting and could lead to a heavy fine, especially in a culture based around honor and shame.

What's so important about that?

The illustration is less about conflict and more about competition. The Greek word *anthistemi* is the basis of the English phrase *not to resist*, but is more accurately translated as *do not compete*.[65]

We should not compete with the world in the way that the world competes.

Before you can truly create a complete path to freedom, you yourself have to be set free from jealousy, insecurity, and the drive to justify yourself.

In the upside down Kingdom of God, winning an enemy over is considered higher than beating one.

Take caution not to think the thoughts that come into your head are merely your own. There are the thoughts of the self, thoughts of the Holy Spirit, and there are thoughts influenced by the spiritual forces of evil in the heavenly realms.

Jesus' comment was about competition.

It is not one.

questions for the pioneer

1. What is being presented to you as the issue? What does your gut instinct tell you the problem really is?

2. Perspective is important. How easily can you take a step back and refocus?

3. Are you taking a knife to a gun fight? If you are, what kind of blade are you trying to use? Intellect? Politics? Something else?

STAGE THREE ✢ RESISTANCE

3

STAGE THREE

RESISTANCE | MY STORY

ethos

One day a ministry with its own internship program approached me, requesting I become its next national director. Pais teams were being planted in more cities. We were starting to flourish. We had gained strength and grown significantly in the level of recognition received from others. It seemed we were being noticed.

Their proposal was for me to take over their program, which at its height had around thirty young people giving a year of their life to serve churches. Rather than seeing Pais as competition, they wanted to join forces. This initially appeared to be a fantastic opportunity with an organization I greatly admired. It had a good-sized platform, annually running several conferences and networking many youth leaders across the country. Our recruitment efforts would inevitably take a giant step forward. There was also the promise of a salary, something that Pais was unable to provide for me. I was excited—this looked like the next obvious step.

But as the saying goes, "The devil is in the details."

As our conversation progressed, the proposal's conditions were unraveled. One stipulated that although I would still be able to run Pais, with these two different styles of courses now under one umbrella, Pais would be required to charge the same amount as those signing up to our 'sister' organization.

I am willing to change many things about Pais. We continuously need to sharpen the presentation of our message within schools. We need to tighten up our recruitment process. The need for change is constantly with us. But one thing I knew then, and still know for sure, is that the Pais apprenticeship should be free for those who join the movement.

Ultimately, the organization and I decided that Pais staying free would not provide a workable partnership. The proposal was amicably dismissed, but a closer connection was made between the two movements.

Throughout the years, Pais has faced many similar decisions, and what has helped us find our way time and time again is our *ethos*.

The more successful Pais appeared to be in our ministry to schools, the more frustrated I personally became about its apparent lack of impact. Pais is merely a means to an end. My vision is to make missionaries, not simply to run programs in schools.

As I have said before, the way Pais works in schools makes sense. But here is the question: Is putting teams into schools enough? It would seem not. As we've grown throughout the years, the bigger picture of reaching young people has become clearer. And, out of this came another wave of awkward questions.

We started to experiment. As my Biblical research deepened, I began to teach more and more on the roots of our faith, the early church, and in particular Jesus' discipleship of his talmidim,[66] many of whom were in their teenage years. My study led to new theories, which led to new philosophies of ministry, which further led to new practices. Subsequently, Pais began a long journey to find churches that would allow us to break traditional systems and try new ways of teaching. We wanted to disciple young people, not simply in schools, but now closer to home…in their youth groups.

We were beginning to tinker, not only with training the children of strangers, but with the children of church parents.

With these new ideas, our ethos developed. We now have core values that stretch beyond the structure of Pais, permeating relationships with churches so that the synergy created can more effectively reach the lost young people of our world.

Ethos is the guiding belief at the very heart of who you are. The more you have, the sharper your vision becomes. However, as with all sharp objects, if not handled correctly, there can be great pain.

m4

I was very much in love with Sharon Church, the church in which I grew up, and I had incredible respect for our pastor, Harry Letson. It was he who, through self-sacrifice and a Kingdom mindset, gave me freedom to build a ministry which went far beyond his church's four walls. Nonetheless, there was a problem: we were quickly out-growing the building. Pais was running its finances under the church's accounts and charitable status, but our conferences could no longer fit within the church's facilities. We needed another building.

Another distinctive about Pais is our economic model. We have never, and ideally will never, own a building of our own. Pais is built on partnership. We provide churches that have established infrastructure and facilities with enthusiastic individuals who possess great leadership skills. Because of my background, I have never learned how to raise a lot of money, but I have learned how to make a little money go a very long way. Here, however, we had a major problem. Virtually every penny of Pais went into people and fuel. Because of our relationship with Sharon Church, we had not needed to raise money for bricks and mortar, but now it seemed we did. Then one day Harry brought to my attention Evangel Church. He had been helping this group of loyal Christians every week by bringing teaching and some pastoral support, but they were still struggling. Their building had been bought when the church was flourishing and growing with two to three hundred people, but was now far larger than the current nineteen members needed. It had some basic structural issues including the proverbial leaking church roof, and they were in the process of selling it to a local restaurant chain.

We asked the church leadership how much they were selling the building for. If my memory serves me right, it was around £180,000.[67] And then they turned to me and made a suggestion. Perhaps, they said, we could sell it to you for our remaining mortgage payments. This, they informed me, was only £46,000.[68]

Some would say this was coincidence and some might say it was God, but £46,000 was exactly to the penny how much money we did not have.

We had nothing. Nada.

The first time I shared the vision, a businessman stepped forward and offered to give me the entire amount. For several reasons however, this did not feel like the right thing to do. Pais owning a building would mean pouring money that could be used for better things into a black hole called 'real estate'.

And then came a new twist. Since the church leaders also felt that selling the building to Pais might not be the best way forward, we settled on a third option.

Pais would lead the church, and we would get the use of the building entirely free.

The church was called Evangel, meaning *good news*, but it could only be good news if people knew its meaning. As we began to re-purpose the church, it started to grow in size. It was an opportunity to try out new ideas, and with this regeneration came a new name. To us, it was far more important for the name to resonate with those outside the building than to be understood inside. Our vision was to impact the community.

We renamed the church 'thefaithworks'.

Some of the people involved in thefaithworks were from the Pais Project. Well over a thousand young people have given their lives for at least a year to serve with Pais. At least 50% of those who originally signed on for one year, committed longer term. Some have even stayed on Pais for a decade. There are, of course, those shining stars that I'll always remember and thank God for their friendship.

Rachel Eden joined Pais when she was 18 years old. She was bright and bubbly, and as she grew on Pais, it became evident that God had given her two skills rarely seen together. Rachel was a drama queen, but in the best sense of the word. She was creative, artsy, and communicated incredibly well through performing arts. Alongside these attributes, Rachel was also very structured, organized, and had a keen strategic mind.

Rachel developed through the ranks from team member to team leader, eventually becoming a director. For several years she ran Street Level, our specialist schools teams that were also mini theatre companies. Eventually Rachel moved to our church in Failsworth and helped pioneer two projects, as she joined Lynn and me in reaching the community. One was Create where, rather than a midweek youth rally of our usual attendees, we put our emphasis on reaching local young people, giving them opportunities to present the gospel through drama.

Most of these young people weren't Christians, but we began to disciple them through the performing arts.

We coached these students to teach others. So, through Create, Pais developed a philosophy that took the form of M4 academy. M4 stood for four ways to make missionaries of the students with whom Pais apprentices connected. The academy became the training ground where they learned to see the Kingdom of God and affect their community positively.

As M4 developed, many academies were launched globally, each one based around the specific skills, gifting, and vision of the apprentices who led them. Through presentational tracks like performing arts, media skills, and public speaking, young people learned how to share the truth of Jesus. Other tracks taught sport skills and created discussion using those skills as spiritual illustrations. My favorite tracks were the service ones. One group of young people went to a local apartment, spoke to the management and posted flyers offering prayer. Residents would write their requests down or visit the team on Wednesday nights and get prayed for.

An Arabian proverb says, *"To teach is to learn twice."*[69]

As students actively engaged in educating both themselves and others, a profound change occurred.

For some, their education turned into an experience. What they were *told* was true, they now *knew* to be true.

For others, their experience turned into an education. What they now knew to be true, they asked to be explained.

Young people who did not initially believe in Christ were invited to be involved in *His* work in *their* communities.

Whenever I speak at conferences, seminaries, or Bible colleges, I often pose the question, "When did the disciples first become Christians?" I typically receive six answers ranging from "When they first followed Him" to "The day of Pentecost". The answer of course is...

...We don't really know.

I then ask the question, "When did Jesus first start to disciple the disciples?"

I receive the unanimous answer, "When they first followed Him."

Simple logic and rational thinking therefore teach us that Jesus discipled many of His followers before they became Christians.[70]

Why then are so many of our church programs traditionally set up to do the exact *opposite*?

The academy was just one quarter of M4. The motto of Pais, *Missionaries making Missionaries*, is represented just as clearly in the other three parts. M4 Mentoring sees our apprentices regularly meet with individual young people for the specific purpose of equipping them to be missionaries in their schools and communities. Within M4 Conferences, students and apprentices receive joint training in everything from setting up a Christian club to serving teachers as Christ would. The last pillar of M4 is Missions. What happens on mission too frequently stays on mission, so Pais does not do mission trips; we do tours. We take young people on tour who are already serving or who want to serve. They get a chance to go into another community and simply do there what they were already doing in their own backyard.

Simply put, what does Pais do?

It sends teams of apprentices into churches. They go into the local schools *as* missionaries and into the youth group to *make* missionaries. Full stop.

But it is not as simple as it sounds.

You may think that going into schools as missionaries creates the problems.

Rather, going into youth groups to make missionaries has provided 90% of the issues that have tested me as a pioneer.

blurred

At thefaithworks, I clearly felt God say to me, *Build a church with blurred edges*. One author correctly stated that God can do anything through a man who does not care who gets the credit.[71] thefaithworks' faith worked because of partnership. Not only did this small church become the home of the Pais Project, but we also partnered with a friend of mine, Andy Hawthorne, pioneer of the Eden Project. This initiative encouraged people to move homes and set up small, healthy communities in the heart of difficult ones.

One of the first things I did when I took on this new role at thefaithworks was talk to Dave, a local policeman. I asked, "What's the worst part of Failsworth?" He replied, "That's simple—Dean Street." I asked him to tell me more.

The initial problem was late night disruption and destruction caused by local gangs. In response, the local residents avoided going out, locking themselves away in their homes. But what came next surprised even me. The gangs had started knocking on doors and when the homeowner answered, they would walk in and order the frightened occupants upstairs. Raiding the fridge, they would then watch TV, do whatever they pleased in the house until the early hours of the morning, and leave a total mess behind.

I sent the proposal for an Eden Project to be set up on Dean Street. The local police responded quickly, saying they had just returned from an emergency meeting about the problems on Dean Street when they found my document on their desk. Plans for Eden quickly developed. Over the next five years, people moved in and bought houses, living their not-so-normal, everyday Christian lives there.

From Pais has evolved another mantra, *People Not Program*. Although we try our best to make our structures and presentations as sharp as possible, we see the vision of Pais as creating a *new kind of person, not a new kind of program*. That statement is the first thing said in one of our promotional videos.

Our firm belief, our ethos, is that what will make an impact is not a well executed system, but a person of passion.

A person who will go the extra mile.

A person to whom the line has become a dot.

So Andy and I began to recruit Eden workers, some of whom had come through Pais networks. Nathan Milnes led the Eden Project in Failsworth. He'd been on Pais as a team member and a team leader. One of the initiative's driving forces was Create.

This concept of a church with blurred edges hoped that people would not be able to see where one program finished and another one started. We hoped that no single organization would get the credit, but that people instead would see the Kingdom come.

Eventually, the Eden Project in Failsworth received an award from the British government due to the radical change in the community. Symbolically, where there had been derelict houses, a garden was planted, and when surveyed by the local government who asked what the garden should be named, some of the residents whose lives had been touched suggested it be called...

Eden.

Although the name was ultimately rejected by the council, it symbolized to us that something of the message had taken root in the hearts of the local community.

The secret to the Eden Project's success was a new kind of person. What made a change was not a whole lot of money being poured in, but a group of young adults who were being trained in how to prove their faith, not protect it. As Pais began to mature, we wanted childlike faith but not childlike minds.

suitcases

I had been part of three churches in my life, and every time I made a change, it was for the sake of what God was doing through Pais. One thing I noticed in my study of the scriptures was that before prophets were able to speak to their nation, they usually had to make some kind of change. For Pais to take its next step, I had to take a next step. I moved to thefaithworks to set up a national center for Pais, but as more and more young people joined Pais from overseas and took it back to their home nations, I was becoming aware that God had put on our hearts what was in fact a global vision. Teams were planted all over England, Northern Ireland, Germany, the USA, and Canada, and were soon to be planted in new continents such as Asia and Africa.

This concept of sparking a global movement grew in my heart and mind.

Once a year I pulled my National Directors together for our Global Summit—a week of fellowship and vision. One decision we addressed in the first couple of years was what kind of organization we wanted to be. Two extremes could fence us in. On one end was the idea of an authoritative legal organization where Pais would be one global non-profit or charity with centralized finances and charitable status. Our concern here was that we would build a static and slow moving institution. On the other end, we knew we could grow very, very quickly if we franchised Pais. I had seen a model in several places whereby local people with a vision had set up a local youth ministry, contacted a national organization, and asked if they could come under their umbrella. The problem here was that in the early days of Pais we had done this on one or two occasions and found that, very quickly, the values, ethos, and principles of Pais were not really evident. It was essentially just people doing schools work. It made *us* look good because we were able to pin more flags in a map, but ultimately we felt it did not make *God* look good as it weakened and diluted the vision.

We chose a third way. We decided to shape the organization through what we called an Apostolic model. This idea was purely based on relationship, respect, and connection. I would have no legal authority in any nation. I could not legally hire or fire, nor determine finances or budget. Instead, we would work on such a strong relational bond that we would flow together in one direction. Leadership would mainly come through a simple process. I would listen and observe what God was doing in each nation. Then after seeking God, I would teach about what needed to be done next. Later, through a mentoring academy I set up, and through meeting online or geographically, we would agree on the practical things that needed to change. A bit like Paul the apostle, I would travel to each nation teaching, advising, asking questions. The Global Summit therefore became hugely important to us. Our informal and admittedly very cheesy motto became *relationship is our office*.

One day while visiting the teams in Texas, I saw a book called *Making Room for Life* by Randy Frazee. At the back of the book was a short description of a church who wanted to really impact its community. It seemed to share similar values to Pais, and I remember telling Tony Puckett, the National Director of Pais:USA at that time, that it might be nice to visit that church one day. I then promptly forgot all about it.

Several months later I received a call from Rebecca Bailey, the National Director of Pais:Canada. At a conference, she heard a speaker share about impacting their community. Afterwards she joined the long line of people waiting to thank him for his insight and words. The minute she began to tell him what she did, he dismissed everyone else in the line and sat her down for a lengthy conversation. His name was Randy Frazee.

Randy and I met so he could share his vision for a *Connecting Church,* a church that would empower its members to live geographically and intergenerationally. After some prayer and discussion, Randy asked if I would consider moving to the States and help re-purpose the student ministry of his church. In turn, he would help us promote Pais on a far bigger platform. In November 2005, Lynn and I packed all we owned into seven suitcases, boarded our sons, Joel and Levi, onto a plane and immigrated to the USA.

The objective was to figure out how the principles of Pais could be implemented in an American mega-church. As I became somewhat of a missionary in a new culture, Randy was a huge proponent and source of encouragement as he helped me think through the problems I would face in America.

A second mantra of Pais, when seeking to impact a community of young people, had become *Process Not Purchase*. As the disciples of Jesus began to take Christ's principles around the world, Peter and John travelled to Samaria where they met a sorcerer named Simon. Simon considered himself a big player and wanted to do the things and see the success that Peter and John were doing and seeing.

> When Simon saw that the Spirit was given at the laying on of the apostles' hands, he offered them money and said, "Give me also this ability."[72]

The curse of resources is that sometimes we think we can purchase or hire the gift of God. Simon, like so many of us, saw success and hoped to take a shortcut to get there. But Peter and John had been on a three-year process.

Sometimes we want to be where people are, but we do not want to walk where they walked to get there.

In this new land of opportunity came a new kind of test. It was like the scene when the young children walk into Willy Wonka's Chocolate Factory. I had boarded a plane and within ten hours went from white trash to white collar, from scarcity to abundance, out of the frying pan and into the fire.

In recent years as my pioneering instinct had grown stronger, I learned to recognize this third stage of resistance.

As Pais began to grow and put teams in different states, our commitment to *process not purchase* created problems. Churches were looking for instant success. The methodology that we were now threatening was one of an attractional ministry. Simply put, the idea appeared to be that you would hire a really cool youth pastor who would put on some really cool programs, resulting in more and more young people flooding into the church building. It would be a reasonably quick process.

Our ethos conflicted with this in several ways.

First, we believed less in heroes and more in heroic teams.

Second, it takes time to build a good reputation within schools. After first serving a community with no strings attached over a period of time, we would begin to win trust, and schools would allow us to spend more time on programs that furthered our message and purpose.

On another note, success for us is not greater numbers *in* the building but greater numbers launched *from* the building. As we will see later, new vision requires new measurements of success. For me, I cannot kid myself into thinking that an attractional ministry would make much of a difference.

Churches are losing incredible amounts of young people every year. Why is that?

One day I came up with a simple phrase which summarized my observations:

Old thinking done really well.

ping pong

As I helped this church repurpose their student ministry, I had to really apply my thinking to how and what we are teaching our young people. I began to realize just how much we dumb down our expectations of what they can achieve. Subsequently, I formed another impression:

Similar thinking done on a different budget.

I had arrived in a world where denominationalism was still strong. In Manchester I had the benefit of seeing churches from various backgrounds working together to reach the youth, but now I was in a stronger Christian culture where doctrinal differences still led to separation. But the paradox I found was that even though many churches were so keen to guard their distinctive beliefs, they were in fact doing the exact same thing!

Where was the variety?! Where were the new ideas?! Where was the creativity?!

In my limited experience of four years in the States, I walked into various churches from Southern Baptist to Pentecostal. What amazed me most was not that they did youth ministry so differently, but that I could not see a single difference at all.

They all had the same kind of program, with the same kind of schedule. They taught the same. They thought the same.

The only difference was that one group had a more expensive ping pong table.

stones

Earlier in the book, I hinted that God does not want to protect pioneers from the test that they must go through.

As Pais began to gain recruits from oversees, I noticed how their different cultures affected their time on Pais. The British apprentices, for instance, were generally less versed in the Bible. Those from Eastern Europe were at times too caught up in the extravagance of their new environment. Germans were hardworking and disciplined, but because many came on Pais due to their mandatory year of National Service, they were less open to stay beyond their initial commitment.

American apprentices generally excelled during our Foundational Training, three weeks of seminary style education at the start of the year. They appeared to know the Bible more, having a greater familiarity with the stories and characters that shaped history, showing a greater tendency towards religious education and study. Two or three months later however, once they started to hit the ground, they struggled to a greater degree than anyone else. It surprised me how difficult they found it to communicate their faith in a secular environment. Many of them struggled to live their faith in a mission field that was predominantly post-Christian.

They seemed to know *what* to believe, but not *how* to believe.

I began to spot a parallel between this quirk of American apprentices and the latest statistics in America. It was estimated that 82% of all students who were actively involved in church before they graduated high school had dropped out of fellowship within the first year of college.[73] Why?

Before David faced Goliath, he had a conversation with his king. He was graciously provided with Saul's own armor for protection. But there was a problem. The problem wasn't what many of us think it was. Sunday school usually paints a picture of a little David in a "big boy's" armor, giving the impression that the armor was physically too large for David. The real issue for David, however, is only brought to light when we understand the original words used. In essence, David turned to Saul and said:

> "I cannot wear this armor because *I have not proven it*."[74]

And for this reason alone, David discarded it.

For many students in the US, they leave their church environment, and like David, they discard the faith of those older than them. David, however, was able to reach for something he had proven—five smooth stones.

As David told Saul, *"Your servant has killed both the lion and the bear."*[75] David was able to do something no one else could do because he reached for something that he had proven.

When US students reach college, they discard the faith of their elders partly due to the fact that they've not proven it. Their bigger problem is that they have nothing else to reach for. Why?

The answer is because we the Church, we their parents, we the system have protected them from every wild animal we possibly can. They face temptation. They face struggle. They face theological challenge. Yet so few of them have stories of when God showed up in their lives because we never allowed them to reach a place where they needed God to show up.

Pioneers need their five smooth stones. They need to commit to a process that does not protect them, but helps them prove God and their vision.

As I began to understand this more, we developed what became another Pais mantra. We call it...

Proving Not Protecting.

We began offering churches some very simple, but slightly different, ideas of what a youth program might look like. A traditional model, both in America and growing throughout the West, appeared to have a mixture of two strong forces. The aforementioned attractional ministry—with entertainment emphasis that was all about making church relevant with video, lighting, and rock bands—mixed with a strong emphasis on Christian education. This method of Bible teaching essentially assumed that if we could fill young people with the Bible when they were young, it would keep them safe during their adult years.

The Jews in the days of Jesus had a similar idea. Their aim was to take young people and 'Stuff them with Torah like an ox.'[76] The problem? Torah means *way*, and yet when the Way, Truth, and Life appeared, they didn't recognize Him.

Our conviction on Pais was to provide students with opportunities to *prove* their faith. We wanted to see students strengthen their education with experience. Not as two separate programs, but merging them together as one.

Pais is in an advantageous position to do this. It has often been said that young people live in two worlds—their weekend Christian world and their weekday school world. Pais, however, has a foot in both of these worlds. Rather than simply educating and sending them out, we want to lead by example in both scenarios.

Yet the Church seems to further define the idea of a separate Christian world. One strange phenomenon sees that during most of the year we protect young people from the world, and yet every so often, maybe during spring break or summer, we send them out—maybe to present the gospel on the streets of a city using performing arts, or perhaps to get down and dirty with a community project in some poverty-stricken area of the world.

We breed hypocrisy.

Our programs, not our hearts nor our philosophy nor our desire nor our structures, helped cement the concept of the two worlds. Pais brings those two things together on a weekly basis—mixing what happens in their school, where they spend much of their waking life, with their church.

Essentially, we empower our young people by giving them at least...five smooth stones.

RESISTANCE || MY STORY

questions for the pioneer

1. What is distinctive about my *it*? How does my *it* make you feel?
2. What is distinctive about your *it*? How might your *it* make others feel?
3. What is there about your *it* that is not up for discussion?

STAGE THREE

RESISTANCE | OUR STORY

bono

Imagine.

Bono, the famous U2 front man and social activist, declares his intention to go into politics. The man's credibility is so huge with the young people of the Western world that virtually every political organization would want him as their representative.

I suspect something similar may have happened with Jesus.

Each religious party may have looked at this young charismatic Rabbi as He first broke onto the scene, hoping that He would be a spokesperson on their behalf.

The Zealots would have been excited. These militant fanatics believed that Israel could be set free if they were just brave enough. They needed a hero to lead them, another David to fight their Goliath. Then they hear the words of Jesus, His promise of a new Kingdom, His descriptions of liberation and freedom. They surge around Him, but one day they watch as Roman soldiers ask Him to move on midway through a public speech. And what does Jesus do? He moves on.

Not their way at all.

The Sadducees and the Herodians however, seeing this, may have been delighted. They wanted to keep their religion but did not want to rock the boat with those who gave them religious power, so looking at Jesus, the phrase 'So far so good!' may have come into their minds. Even better, they hear Him tell their disciples, "If a Roman soldier tells you to carry his bag, go the extra mile," but then Jesus uses inflammatory language. He seems to hint that He is the Messiah, maybe even God. The Messiah was one who promised a free people, a god could not be tolerated by Caesar who thought he was a god himself. When asked to quiet His tone, what does He do? He does not back down.

Not their way at all.

This young Rabbi's attitude towards materialism and community would have thrilled the Essenes, a group who had long-since rejected the worldliness of the

Jews inhabiting Jerusalem. They set up their communities in the hills, and now these 'Sons of Light' were waiting for the Messiah who would surely recognize that they were the chosen ones. And yet Jesus did not simply wander in the wilderness as John had done. When seeing the worldliness around Him, what does He do? He engages all the more.

Not their way at all.

Finally the Pharisees. It was with this religious sect that Jesus had the most in common. Only of the Pharisees did Jesus say to His disciples, "Do what they teach." These interpreters of the law, many of whom sat in Moses' seat, seemed to have an ally in this man who preached purity and shared their hopes of an Israel free from sin. Was this their man? Was this motivational teacher the one who could carry their thoughts and their actions all the way? And yet one day, a Pharisee hears singing and laughter coming from a local home. Looking through a window, he sees Jesus side by side with the sinners—the prostitute, the tax collectors, or let me put it another way, the pedophile and the homosexual. When asked to judge the sinner, what does He do? He forgives all the more.

Not their way at all.

resistance

As Jesus moves to the third stage of pioneering, He encounters a new challenge. Not only did the Zealots, Sadducees, Essenes, and Pharisees have high expectations of Him, but pressure also began to come from many other places:

> *After the people saw the miraculous sign that Jesus did, they began to say, "Surely this is the Prophet who is to come into the world." Jesus, knowing that they intended to come and make him king by force, withdrew again to a mountain by himself.*[77]

The third stage of pioneering is resistance.

You have probably heard the expression, "If you can't beat them, join them." Well I have a new twist on that. I would say that you will one day face those who think to themselves, "If you can't beat them, get them to join you."

Resistance is required from pioneers.

Those who at first did not see *it* and therefore did not believe in *it,* later became threatened by *it* but hoped *it* would go away.

These people are now faced with the realization that *it* is here to stay.

The popularity of Jesus was growing, and it seemed like an inevitable wave of hysteria was about to carry this young Rabbi to the very top. Those in authority, with an agenda camouflaged by power, status, and title, try another tactic. They approach the Pioneer and now offer all that they previously withheld. As we will see later, Satan himself comes out from the shadows and offers Jesus the world if He will only compromise. But Jesus resists.

As I have said before, to advance the Kingdom, pioneers have to go the extra mile rather than dwell on the line. The line, remember, represents the path that has already been trodden. It has been created, established, resourced, and approved. You see that something new needs to happen. But you will be tempted to conform to what already is. You will be presented with the opportunities and resources that you previously sought, but they will come at a price.

The price is compromise.

My hope is that you break through this stage and keep running, empowered not by a vision of vision, but by a vision of God. And then, when you look back over your shoulder, the line will have become a dot to you.

easy

For us as pioneers to keep moving on our journey and not fail in the third stage, we need to be equipped with three principles.

First comes definition.

As Pais developed in other nations, I began to make more transatlantic flights which resulted in me becoming, I confess, a plane snob. When booking flights, I now consider the particular airline offering the trip. The lowest price is still my priority, but I prefer to travel with certain airlines. Some airlines have better service. Some have little televisions that play looping movies in the back of the seat in front of you. Others go the extra mile, offering multiple movies, plus the ability to pause, rewind, and fast forward. The choice of snacks varies as well. I know which airlines provide my favorite English delights free of charge—chunky Kit Kats, Cornish Pasties, and English breakfasts. Even the quality of the little travel packs they give you can make my day. My favorite airline gives me a free toothbrush and woolly socks.

One Saturday night several years ago, I was travelling from Manchester to Belfast in Northern Ireland. Booking a quick flight on a no-frills airline called Easy Jet, I flew out of Liverpool accompanied by a huge army of Irish Manchester United fans who had just come from a big match. The atmosphere in the airport was chaotic. A gang even tried to start a fight with me as I walked into the restroom. However, the most extraordinary thing on that flight was the 'welcome' by the flight attendant who tried to communicate amidst a roar of football chants, expletives, and general pandemonium. I cannot recall her precise words but this was almost exactly what she said:

> *Listen, you lot! We've already contacted the Belfast police. If you give us any trouble, we'll have you locked away! Don't touch me. Don't speak to me.*

With a few quick points to the back and the side (indicating to, I believe, the exits) she concluded her motivational speech:

> *Now shut up and belt up!*

I just sat there. I would like to have gone to the restroom, but I couldn't take the risk.

I looked around the plane with a wry smile on my face: I had missed England. Then I noticed something strange. I was not in any way disappointed. There were no TVs or travel packs, and I had to pay for my chunky Kit Kat. But still, I was not disappointed.

Why?

Because this particular airline had clearly defined itself. It promised only two things: to be cheap, which it was; and to get me there on time, which it did. Easy Jet's brand was clear and simple—*We aim to be the cheapest and most reliable. But don't expect top level frills.*

Pioneers need to understand the importance of defining themselves. Definition has two benefits. It tells people what they should not expect from us. This releases us from unrealistic pressure to spend time on things that distract us from our main purpose.

And, definition holds us accountable. This is especially important as we find ourselves in not only uncharted territory, but unstructured territory as well. We create our own schedules. We decide our programs. We have to be the ones that initiate. For some pioneers this can be dangerous, because if we lose sight of our vision of God that drives us, we may fall into simply managing rather than pioneering. We slowly, inconspicuously, and without forethought crawl back into our comfort zone. Publicly defining ourselves puts the right kind of pressure on us to fulfill what we say we must.

I was around thirty-five years old when I came to the understanding of who I am. I'm not simply talking about my identity in Christ, but my God-given purpose and mission in life.

Simply stated:

I make missionaries.

This frees me up.

When I was asked to lead what became thefaithworks church in England, I clearly communicated this to them. I would not be leading the church as a pastor. Therefore, I would not spend a great deal of time visiting people to talk about their aches and pains, not that this was not needed, but they did not need me to do that. I would not be the primary person creating Bible studies or organizing inspirational events. All of these are useful and I have the ability to do them, but none of them should be my priority. In advance, as we discussed what a church partnered and led by Pais would look like, an understanding developed. I would lead by making missionaries. I would invest heavily in those leaning forward, not in those with complaints.

It is a wonderful feeling when you are released to be who you are.

Notice I do not say *when you are released to do what you want to do.* All pioneers have to roll up their sleeves and get involved. In the early stages of pioneering, we have to do almost everything.[78]

On the other hand, the church was able to hold me accountable for the things I said I would bring. Empowerment. Inspiration. Mentoring. Coaching. The fruit they would see, I told them, would be a church that was active in the community. Our vision was to create a group of God's people that was such good news to their neighbors that, if for any reason it disbanded, those in the local community would wave banners and walk along the streets protesting, "Save Our Church!"

I want to encourage you as a pioneer to ask God to give you an understanding of yourself, to give you definition.

triangle

Second comes distinction.

It is paramount that we recognize what makes our vision original and unique. With the Pais Project, schools ministry has not done that for us. Such organizations are on school campuses around the world. Many are living life with young people, sharing their faith, and doing an amazing job of expanding the Kingdom of God into the schools of their nations.

Several things do make Pais distinctive though. Our apprenticeships are free. We partner with local churches. We place our apprentices within host homes. We believe in intergenerational ministry.

However, there is one thing more than anything else that makes us distinctive, one thing that is a priority to us.

Pais is not about a new kind of *program*, but about a new kind of *person*.

> In the past he humbled the land of Zebulun and the land of Naphtali, but in the future he will honor Galilee of the Gentiles, by the way of the sea, along the Jordan— The people walking in darkness have seen a great light; on those living in the land of the shadow of death a light has dawned.[79]

The 'Way of the Sea' that Isaiah mentions runs through Capernaum and was an international highway in Jesus' time.[80] The prophet also mentions two Jewish tribal lands, Zebulun and Naphtali. While Nazareth was located in the tribal area of Zebulun, Capernaum fell within the ancient tribal boundaries of Naphtali. Jesus exactly fulfilled the prophet's words by spending His boyhood in Zebulun and much of His ministry in Naphtali.

Have you ever wondered where Jesus recruited His disciples from?

Jesus grew up in Nazareth surrounded by friends and fellow Jews. He had family there and others who, we find out later, were eager to hear His words. Do you know how many people lived in Nazareth while Jesus was there? Around 300. It was familiar...

But Jesus did not choose any of His disciples from there.

Around three miles away was Tzippori. This was a fast growing, extremely modern city for that time. It started to grow in 2 BC and not long afterwards, 25,000 lived there. It was a place of culture, called the *Ornament of Galilee*, and hosted the Mona Lisa of the Middle East: a beautiful Greek mosaic. Some believe that one of Jesus' grandparents came from this city. Influenced by Greek culture during Jesus' time, one of the outstanding things of Tzippori was the theatre which was hugely popular and held 4,500 people. Just think—one single place of entertainment that held 15 times the number of people that were in Jesus' hometown.

We know that Jesus was a *tekton*, a builder or artisan. If you were a young man working in your father's business and your hometown only had 300 homes, but within eyesight was a huge metropolis, where do you think you may have done a lot of your work? Although none of the four accounts of Jesus' life specifically mention that Jesus went to Tzippori, common sense and some indirect information lead us to believe that He certainly did. Not only did He have ancestral links and job opportunities, but in that theater of Tzippori were actors known as *hypocrites*. Jesus is the only Person in the entire New Testament to give people that label. Did He call people *play actors* because He was familiar with the theater? No rabbi would set foot in such a place, but they would set foot in such a city. Also, Tzippori was the administrative center for the king, and Jesus recruited Joanna, the wife of Herod's finance minister, as one of His fiscal supporters. If Jesus needed politicians to organize His ministry, or actors who were great communicators, or businessmen and executives who could skillfully manage a financial support campaign, Tzippori would have been the place to go.

But Jesus did not choose any of His disciples from there.

Fifteen miles away from Nazareth in the opposite direction of Tzippori, stood Beth Shan. Another large city, it boasted a theater, an arena, and a university. If Jesus had wanted cool athletes who would attract large crowds or great thinkers to work through the contemporary issues of His message, He would have chosen disciples from Beth Shan.

But He did not.

Instead, Jesus went to a little town called Fishington. We know it as Bethsaida.

This small town had around 600 people comprised of maybe eight to ten extended families. There was no theater or stadium. No gymnasium or political center. Yet five of Jesus' disciples came from this tiny village. Their names were Peter, Andrew, James, John, and Phillip.[81]

Jesus, so it seems, was looking for a particular type of person.

Bethsaida was part of what is known as the Orthodox Triangle, a very small area with three villages at its corners—Bethsaida, Capernaum, and Korazin. Eighteen of Jesus' 33 recorded miracles were performed here on the northern beaches of the Sea of Galilee. According to some historians, all of the twelve disciples came from this area, with the possible exception of Judas.[82] A particularly passionate type of religious Jew lived in the Orthodox Triangle, and it was here that Jesus went on a search for those who would extend the path He pioneered.

Certain things distinguished people from this area—a strong desire to understand Torah and a fascination with the concept of the Kingdom of God.

They were also distinguished by their strong belief in discipleship.

steamboat

Steamboat Springs is in the Rocky Mountains and is the training ground and home of many USA ski Olympians. It is said that if you want to be a champion winter Olympian, you need to train with the best. And the most experienced coaches are found in Steamboat Springs.

In the same way, if you wanted to excel in your understanding of Torah and were dedicated to living it out, you would go where many of the great rabbis lived. You would go to the Orthodox Triangle. In Korazin, for instance, remains one of the few synagogues that still have a Moses' seat, the place where the scripture would be read. As one historian[83] points out, there is a difference between students and talmidim (the word for disciples).

Students wanted to *know* what their rabbi *knew*.

Talmidim wanted to *be* who their rabbi *was*.

Although a lack of faith was often demonstrated in this area, the other end of the pendulum also existed. This was the home of young idealists, visionaries, those who were leaning forward. Jesus came here to find people of peace.

Jesus did not go into the world to introduce a new kind of program, but instead introduced the world to a new kind of person. He took these twelve talmidim from their homes, and after spending three years as their Rabbi, He sent them from Jerusalem to Samaria, and the ends of the earth.

When approached by a potential disciple of approximately fourteen years old, a rabbi would ask himself some big questions: "Can this disciple be like me? Can he live like me? Can he teach like me? Will people follow him as they've followed me?"

"Will he be able to pass on my *yoke*?"

A rabbi's yoke was partly his teaching, but much more than that. It was a compilation of his interpretations of the Torah. A rabbi would look at the law and study the law and determine the practical applications to every area of life—including eating, and working, and even relieving oneself in the restroom.[84]

Jesus said, *"My yoke is easy."*[85] What He meant by this was that a new kind of person would worship in spirit and truth. Those who followed Him would be less dictated by laws (although they still would fulfill the Torah) and more led by the Spirit.

In the same way, Pais has what you may consider a 'yoke'. Our foundational teaching aims to produce a very real and authentic missionary. At the core of this teaching is a series entitled *The Kingdom Principles*. The book yet to be written, which encompasses the teaching on Kingdom principles, will be called *The Line and the Cloud*. This book you are reading, *The Line and the Dot*, is a compilation of a different series called *The Kingdom Pioneers*. Whereas *The Kingdom Pioneers* looks at vision, *The Kingdom Principles* studies character. These principles of Pais shape a new kind of missionary.

Valuing this distinctive is a key weapon in our fight to resist compromise. I want to always be able to look out at a group of young Pais missionaries and think to myself:

"I believe in *you* as much as I believe in *it*."

tape

Third comes defense.

To equip us for this third stage of pioneering, we have to understand there is something to defend...but what is it?

Some things can be compromised in order to grow. The key you will need is not simply a defense against compromise, but instead an understanding of what things you can make concessions on and what things you must not give up.

The thing you need to protect is the thing that made you unique!

All pioneers need to ask, "What was it that made us different in the first place?" Once you have defined that, then make it distinctive, give it value, and then defend it.

How do you defend the one thing that made you unique? It all comes down to how you measure success.

Measuring success is like creating a tape measure, looping it at the end and forming a leash. I know one church, for instance, whose stated vision is about getting people out of the church into the community, but their only measurement of success is the mathematics of counting the numbers who attend on a Sunday morning. No matter how much the senior minister tries to push outward and bring the church with him, this measuring leash jerks him back and forces him to spend most of his time ensuring the Sunday morning program is attractive enough to draw greater numbers.

What measurement has become your leash?

flags

I have to believe in the people of Pais. This has meant slower growth than could have been possible otherwise. I am one of those men who has that inward drive to stick flags in maps, but I have had to resist the urge to compromise.

And so for a season, I have had to commit myself to those awkward conversations with churches who would give us the world if we simply provided interns. It has become apparent to me that Pais can flourish at a tremendous rate and receive finances I could probably not dream of if we simply get into the business of providing cheap labor to churches. If the vision was simply to provide communities with nice young people who were enthusiastic, then my life would be simpler and our reputation far bigger.

But it is not.

questions for the pioneer

1. I 'make missionaries'. The vision of Pais is *Missionaries Making Missionaries*. How might you succinctly and distinctly define and theme your vision in a short sentence?

2. What should people expect and not expect from you? How could you encourage and discourage them to do this?

3. What are the old measurements of success? What do the new measurements of success need to be for this new vision? What one thing makes your vision unique? This is what you must protect.

STAGE THREE

RESISTANCE | YOUR STORY

purity

Have you ever thought about the pressure to perform that Jesus must have felt?

> Then Jesus was led by the Spirit into the desert to be tempted by the devil. After fasting forty days and forty nights, he was hungry. The tempter came to him and said, "If you are the Son of God, tell these stones to become bread."
>
> Jesus answered, "It is written: 'Man does not live on bread alone, but on every word that comes from the mouth of God.' "
>
> Then the devil took him to the holy city and had him stand on the highest point of the temple. "If you are the Son of God," he said, "throw yourself down. For it is written:
> > " 'He will command his angels concerning you,
> > and they will lift you up in their hands,
> > so that you will not strike your foot against a stone.' "
>
> Jesus answered him, "It is also written: 'Do not put the Lord your God to the test.' "
>
> Again, the devil took him to a very high mountain and showed him all the kingdoms of the world and their splendor. "All this I will give you," he said, "if you will bow down and worship me."
>
> Jesus said to him, "Away from me, Satan! For it is written: 'Worship the Lord your God, and serve him only.' "
>
> Then the devil left him, and angels came and attended him." [86]

Jesus lived with the purpose of making *true* disciples...Talmidim.

There were twelve young men; some scholars believe the youngest could have been nine years old.

Only an initial twelve. Imagine the pressure He may have been under for 'good numbers'.

Pais no longer measures converts, we measure disciples. For many years, team leaders would report how many young people had responded to some kind of altar call.

Altar calls, of course, never existed in Jesus' time. It was not until the eighteenth century that our Christian faith became individualized and words such as *personal Savior* became popular. During the 1950s, the altar call became famous through a great evangelist.[87]

But Jesus did not say, "Go and make converts." He told us to "Go and make disciples."[88]

So, rather than measure converts, we measure integration—how many young people join us as we join with the whole family of God?

Jesus also had an integration target—the whole world.

I am quite sure the devil knew the pressure to perform that was upon Him. "I'll give you the world," he said.

The test you as a pioneer will face in this third stage of resistance is to conform. Because of pressure from many places, we feel the need to compromise in order to gain resources, a need reinforced by our desire to compete and conform.

But conformity comes with a price. That price is best summed up in the definition of compromise:

> *A settlement of a dispute in which two or more sides agree to accept less than they originally wanted.*[89]

Some strive for quality above quantity; others target quantity before quality. However, I believe the quest of a pioneer is for purity—purity of vision. To advance the mission of Pais, I need to ensure that the principles of Pais are fully adopted and our practices are purely connected to what makes us original and distinctive.

Purity leads to quality; quality leads to quantity.

promotion

When tempted by the devil, Jesus was offered everything He knew would ultimately come, but in the form of a shortcut—*shortcut* being another definition of the word *compromise*.

We compromise for various reasons. One reasons is that the resources we need are not available. But there are also other pressures waiting to ambush us. They seek to fence us in and cause us to withdraw back to the 'line'.

Earlier I told the story of the church I led in Manchester. If you remember, I agreed to lead the church so that Pais could use its building and we could model a fellowship of making missionaries. As part of my denomination's practice, I had an induction ceremony whereby I was officially ordained as the minister. Various friends, family members, and local leaders gathered with the very small congregation of 19 adult believers. Many of those present were connected with the Pais Project, which at that time was reaching over 200,000 students in the schools of England.

On that day an incident occurred which, although in no way dramatic, significantly disturbed me.

I'll always remember walking through the door into the main meeting area. People turned to greet me and smile, and one particular older lady walked up to me. She had been a supporter of Pais and followed my ministry for some time. She was aware of the impact we were having in the local schools, and truly no one else in the room wanted to encourage me more. As she approached, she laid her hand on my arm and looked into my eyes. After a moment she uttered words that would occupy my mind throughout the duration of the ceremony:

"Paul, I always knew that someday you would be promoted!"

What? Promoted?

I simply could not understand what she had said and certainly could not get my mind around it. Here was a woman who loved Jesus, loved Pais, and was what many of us would consider a mature and well-discipled follower of Christ. And yet how could it be that, in her mind, looking after 19 adults who were already Christians was a *promotion* from reaching 200,000 students, 99% of which had never been given an opportunity to respond to the gospel, and many had not even heard it?

Status.

Nothing will limit our desire to change the world more than the sin of pride. I have probably lost track of the number of good leaders I have lost because actions speak louder than words.

And by actions, I mean cash.

Why did this lady think that being a pastor was more valuable than reaching so many young people? The answer is simple: she had been taught this her entire Christian life. No one had said to her, "A pastor of few is greater than someone involved in schools ministry." But where money is spent, value is added.

Even now as the Founding Director of Pais, I could without question earn more money pastoring an average-sized church. This was not the issue of one old lady; it's the mindset of modern Christianity. I have had great leaders on Pais who were seeing God do amazing things in their lives and in the lives of the students with whom they worked. Yet, despite this obvious approval by God, many asked me to change their 'title'. In their eyes, I could see the pressure they felt for validation. Interestingly, the pressure is not from the secular world around them, but from the very Christian sub-culture in which they live and work. Even my closest friends have implied, at times, these leaders should get a 'proper' job.

As a pioneer, you must resist the temptation to conform in order to go to the next level. Your defense against the pressure to compromise is…

Faith.

megamix

Before the dawn of Pais, there was Megamix. In England we have six weeks of summer vacation from schools, and during that time, many children get in trouble because the devil always finds work for idle hands. So, Lynn and I pioneered an idea we called Megamix. For £1 a day, we would take children off the street and create a whole day of activity. There would be games, crafts, trips out, and a whole hour of teaching about Jesus.

Our first Megamix consisted of Lynn, myself, and around thirty children. But over a period of four years, it grew to over 100 children between the ages of 3-14. Out of 100 'megamixers,' seven or eight of them may have come from Christian families. I recruited volunteers who gave their entire summer to this local mission.

The plan was simple. Every day, Monday through Friday, every week for six weeks, we created the best summer we possibly could for these children, most of whom came from families who couldn't afford any type of recreation, much less family vacations. For seven hours a day, we built relationships, and for one of those hours, we shared our faith through story, performing arts, and song. Even fifteen years later, adults approach me on the streets to tell me how it impacted them as children. One young man became a British boxing champion, and the last time I saw him, he asked if he could bring his children to Megamix.

To say that we flew by the seat of our pants is an understatement. We had no idea what we were doing, but were led entirely by common sense, creative thinking, and desperation for God's Spirit to empower us. Megamix had no funding. The six-week-program for 100 children operated on a total of £500 which was provided by the parents who could afford to give us £1 a day.

It demanded some creative thinking.

We raised extra money from our snack shop, and I did all I could to get the children to spend their pocket money there rather than at the local corner shop.

Desperate times call for desperate measures. I remember a field trip where I took 100 children up a local mountain and forced them to carry the snack shop up there, knowing they would be incredibly thirsty by the time we reached the summit. By then, the nearest competition was several miles away, so of course we sold out of soda pop within three minutes.

Looking back, I'm quite confident most of our creative ideas were probably illegal or, at the very least, defied an abundance of health and safety guidelines.

One area where this became evident was the whole realm of discipline. How do you keep 100 street kids well-behaved for an entire day when most of that day is spent doing as many crazy and fun things to get them excited as you possibly can? The answer is simple—torture. Now, when I say 'torture,' please know I mean things that would seem torturous to *them*. I would find little cubby holes and places where I could make them sit during 'time out'. Sometimes it was simply under the church piano or on the stairs. But I have to admit I would occasionally forget where I placed some of them, only to stumble upon them an hour later on the way to my office. Unsurprisingly, sometimes things backfired.

You have to realize we are not talking about normal children here. Some of these kids from Moston (a rough area in Manchester) had kind of warped minds. I tried everything to force them to behave. There was the *water torture*, which involved a kid holding a bowl of water above his own head until he could no longer hold it and it poured over him. There was also something we affectionately named the *onion torture*, a particular favorite of mine. This involved chopping up ten onions, putting them in a plastic bowl, forcing the head of the naughty youngster into the bowl with them, and putting a dish towel over them. I'll never forget the day a young boy lifted his head, eyes streaming with tears, and every other boy, and some of the girls, screamed at me, "Let me have a go! Please let me have a go!" The *onion torture*, the *light a match and stick it in your mouth for as long as you can torture*, and many others would often backfire. Eventually, they all became games.

But Megamix bent some other rules which led to its eventual end.

Torture aside, the reputation of Megamix grew. More parents brought their young people, and more children walked off the street to join us. This led to a meeting with the local government. Megamix was by far the largest summer club in our part of Manchester, and therefore they wanted to help fund it. At first, this injection of cash came with no strings attached.

This is where we made a fundamental error. I never asked the awkward questions. I simply thanked them, and with my desire to reach as many young people as I could, I went on my way with a friendly smile. The extra funding allowed us to create additional activities and improve the services that Megamix offered. We could buy resources and even cover some volunteer expenses.

But it came with a price.

> *No one can serve two masters. Either he will hate the one and love the other, or he will be devoted to the one and despise the other. You cannot serve both God and money.*[90]

The local government began to tighten up on the Christian ministry that we provided. Most of the parents were more than happy about what we taught. Their attitude was, "I may not go to church, but I love the fact that my children do." But apparently, we were breaking the rules. After a site visit, the government officials pulled the funding.

It might seem we could simply revert to what we originally did, but by this point, we were so reliant upon the financial backing that going back to the previous budget was impossible. The parents couldn't afford to give more money, and eventually we pulled the plug. Years later, I'm still not convinced this was the right thing to do.

I learned a number of lessons from this experience, but the most important here is my mistake in thinking that *ignorance is bliss*. When offered the money, I should have asked those awkward questions, but my thinking was distorted by my drive to see children impacted by God, His Word, and His people.

Pioneers, dreamers, visionaries, those with a hope in your hearts, let me encourage you to never stop asking those awkward questions and always, always, always look a gift horse straight in the mouth.[91]

custard

Faith comes through hearing, and *faith* is what is needed to ask difficult questions.

Faith is not just required for stepping out but also, and especially, for waiting. In between the moment you decide to go the extra mile and the moment the vision is realized, you will get nervous and anxious while waiting.

> *So do not worry, saying, 'What shall we eat?' or 'What shall we drink?' or 'What shall we wear?'*[92]

The Greek word here translated as worry is *merimnao*. It means *to divide into parts* or quite literally to *go to pieces*. It is in the waiting that you will most likely to be tempted to compromise. One way this compromise can manifest itself is by causing you to look back on what 'worked' in the past because you know it's a sure fire way to get the resources you need. If you have faith however, you will attract God's provision.

To have faith is not to dictate *how* God can provide.

I had not yet recruited the first team and we did not have transport. For most of my solo years, I walked to the various schools. The first school I worked in took 50 minutes to get to; I held a 25 minute lunch time club, and then would walk 50 minutes back home. Another school I served entailed a one-way commute of an hour and ten minutes. All this added up to a very fit pioneer, but a lot of wasted time.

Eventually I was able to buy bus tickets which cut down the commuting time a little. But after a couple years of doing this (and with the aim of having a whole team with me), I needed to step out and buy a car. With faith the size of a mustard seed, I bought the smallest car I possibly could. It was a Fiat Biz. Apparently 'Biz' is the Italian word for *reborn* or *born again*. I thought it might be a sign. Lynn also needed transport as she was trying to raise money as a mobile hairdresser. This car was so economical that she bought one for her mini business. Hers was red and mine was yellow and so we nicknamed them 'Jelly' and 'Custard'. I took out a loan to buy this car, hoping that somehow God would provide for the need.

A few days later I met Kevin Pimblott, mentioned earlier on, who blessed us with finances from a grant. God had provided the money for Custard.

But that was not the end.

After a year or so of the smallest car in Britain carrying the first Pais team of five members around the schools of North Manchester day in and day out, it finally gave up the ghost. This, of course, created a problem. We had no money to buy another car, and so I sadly handed the keys over to a friend who said he could get maybe £50 for scrap metal. A few hours later he called. Apparently, as he was driving in to the salvage yard, another car drove into the back of him and totaled it. He was fine, and a few days later I received a check from the insurance company for almost the full amount I had paid for the car.

That is the story of Custard's last stand.

house

Once we were married, Lynn and I moved into an area near our church. It was not the nicest area we could have moved to, but we wanted to be where our skills best met the need. It was the area where most of the Megamix kids lived. The few streets that surrounded us were difficult and rough—remember this was the area a national newspaper called "a ghetto of underprivileged underachievers".[93]

Over a period of five years there, the area became more violent. I constantly broke up fights and on several occasions brought bloodied people into our home to bandage their wounds. Because of our low income and my complete lack of handyman skills, our house had deteriorated further. There was mold on the walls, and ice on the inside of the windows in wintertime. We had no central heating, no double glazing (double-paned windows), and no alarm system.

Several friends encouraged us not to continue with Pais, suggesting several opportunities for well-paid positions at local churches. With a simple phone call it seemed, I could strike a deal with another party where we would both get less than what we originally hoped: I would be doing something *similar* to what God had told me, and they would hire an enthusiastic, but ultimately frustrated, staff member.

To cap it all, one night a particularly bad storm blew off several of our house's roof tiles. We asked our insurance company for repair money, but they told us that it was normal wear and tear and we would need around £2000[94] to fix the problem.

We prayed.

Again, this is where so many would-be pioneers opt for the *similar* route. Almost the vision, but not quite. It is said, "Never cut a tree down in wintertime." There may be no leaves on the branches, nothing green, nothing flowering, and no fruit. It may even appear dead. But under the surface, it is still alive. Never cut down your vision in times of trouble. Never restrict it or limit it for a *similar* route that provides instant resources. There may be some reading even now who have done exactly this. It's not an easy place to be.

A couple of weeks after we prayed, we received a letter from the local government informing us that some houses in the area would receive small grants for house alarms and help with re-roofing. It was just a few weeks after Susan's murder. During the investigation, the police had set up a mobile unit. The heavy police presence over the following weeks caused those involved in criminal activity to move out. Within the space of two weeks, one third of the residents in that small area had moved away. In an attempt to keep what the local authorities called the 'respectable residents,' they had found some European money to pour into the area. A couple of days later, an inspector turned up on our doorstep. He informed us we could get some help to re-roof and a grant for an alarm system. What he said next, however, was particularly interesting. He said that, one street away, residents were receiving grants of up to £12,000.[95] Residents would have to pay 10%, but these grants were given in order to raise the standard of living in the community.

Now, what I did not know was Lynn had taken it upon herself to lay her hands on the walls of our house and pray for healing. Although to me this seemed an odd thing to do, I certainly could not argue at the results.

We prayed again.

Two weeks later, the local government informed us that the boundaries had moved and we were now inside the eligible area. To cut a long story short, they first told us after an inspection that they could give us £16,000[96] to help with damp-proofing and other necessities. They then means-tested us, appraising exactly how much could be provided in grant funds.

They told us we wouldn't have to contribute one penny.

As work was done, more issues came up, and then through some poor decision making, they eventually decided to knock the entire house down and rebuild it from scratch. They totally redesigned our house. They got rid of the mold, installed central heating and double glazed windows and, believe it or not, added an extra bedroom. Eventually they spent £62,000.[97] The only original structures remaining were one wall and the floor.

Unfortunately though, they could not fit in the Jacuzzi I had most politely requested.

I share these stories to encourage you to hold firm to the things which make your vision unique.

you

> *As the time approached for him to be taken up to heaven, Jesus resolutely set out for Jerusalem.*[98]

When I hear the word *resolutely* it brings to mind a man who has had a discussion, thought it through, come to a conclusion, and made a decision. The conversation is now over.

Jesus, the ultimate Pioneer, the one Hebrews tells us to fix our eyes on, was uncompromising.

He was uncompromising in His attitude towards those He considered followers:

> *He who is not with me is against me, and he who does not gather with me scatters.*[99]

He was uncompromising in His expectations of His disciples:

> *Jesus said to him, "Let the dead bury their own dead, but you go and proclaim the kingdom of God."*[100]

He was uncompromising in His teaching:

> *From this time many of His disciples turned back and no longer followed Him.*[101]

He was uncompromising concerning those He would call His own:

> *If anyone is ashamed of me and my words in this adulterous and sinful generation, the Son of Man will be ashamed of him when he comes in his Father's glory with the holy angels.*[102]

He was uncompromising when accused:

> *When he was accused by the chief priests and the elders, he gave no answer. Then Pilate asked him, 'Don't you hear the testimony they are bringing against you?' But Jesus made no reply, not even to a single charge—to the great amazement of the governor.*[103]

He was uncompromising regarding forgiveness:

> *But if you do not forgive men their sins, your Father will not forgive your sins.*[104]

Take comfort that all hell was thrown at Jesus to stop Him from dying for you.

But He did not compromise.

Most historians agree Jesus was submitted to the infamous *forty lashes minus one*. Before His crucifixion, a whip, the ends of which had pieces of bone and metal sewn into them, was lashed across his back, wrapping itself around His waist and chest. The most grueling part was not the way the instrument of torture hit the skin, but the mutilation created as it was pulled away. When extracted, the pieces of metal and bone tore and sliced His flesh so that when the torture was over, the flesh would have been peeled away, exposing His vital organs through His back.

There were three types of stakes the Romans used for crucifixion. There was the 'X', there was the 'T', and there was the cross. Traditionally the third type, the cross, was used if a transcription was to be placed above the victim:

> *This is Jesus. King of the Jews.*[105]

After crucifixion, bodies were often left to be eaten by wild beasts, but not in the case of the Jews. To placate them, the Romans allowed their bodies to be buried immediately after death. Because of this, they would speed the death of Jews on the cross either by kindling a fire beneath them, letting wild beasts attack them while still dying, or by breaking their bones with an iron mallet.

Jesus knew He was facing one of these unspeakable acts.

As a child, Jesus would have likely witnessed the 2000 rebels crucified by the Romans in one day just up the road from Nazareth in the city of Sepphoris.[106]

According to *Foxes' Book of Martyrs*, people on their way to crucifixion were so unspeakably terrified, and often became so pale that they appeared to be ghosts. Others, sick with fear, lost use of their legs, the ability to speak, and even their minds.

But Jesus did not compromise. If He was uncompromising then, He is uncompromising now. He will not compromise concerning you.

He will never accept less than He originally wanted…

You.

storm

God rarely provides before an individual steps out.

Perhaps this is why there are so few pioneers. Many individuals have a vision, a dream, or a sense of distinct purpose. But they are waiting for things to fall into place, giving them the freedom to go and do what they have been told. These individuals are waiting, not just for a hidden word, but for hidden provision—provision which will stay hidden unless they break away.

A couple of years ago, it became clear to me I should fully launch myself into Pais. We had teaching and resources that needed to be taught on a wider scale. But since so little was known about Pais at the time, and because I was convinced of its mission, I knew it was necessary to spend the majority of my time and energy promoting Pais. I worked out a plan with the church I was employed at, and we agreed on a long, almost one-year transition out of my role. I was to go full-time for Pais.

There was only one small hindrance to this calling: since the economic model of Pais had always been to work through the local church and thereby be supported financially, leaving the church position and running Pais full-time would mean I had *no salary*.

One day, a few weeks before my salary from the church ended, I was speaking in Monument, Colorado. Secretly, as many people in my position do, I hoped for a large attendance at church that day. More people mean a better chance to find one or two who may catch the vision of Pais and therefore be led to support us financially. In spite of my hope, a huge blizzard (huge even for Colorado) 'happened' to hit the area. As I looked around the church that morning, I was greatly disheartened. Their usual gathering of 800 people had depleted to 60 or 70. I remember asking God the question, "Why? I know You believe in what I'm doing, so why bring me here on the one Sunday when no one is around?"

It just so 'happened' another couple with whom I had stayed once before and who lived in Steamboat Springs, the very city I was to visit next, was in Colorado Springs for the weekend on a family getaway. Despite the storm, they 'happened' to visit the church where I was preaching that morning. Since they were heading back home to Steamboat Springs right after church, they offered to give me a ride.

Anyone familiar with the Rocky Mountains will know the traffic involved when a big winter storm hits. This trip, which should have taken about four hours, took eight. What should have been a very stressful drive, turned out to be quite fun. I was amused with their young children who, with their various antics and funny questions and comments, kept us entertained.

During this God-appointed journey, my acquaintances became friends. They said they had listened to various recordings of my teachings over the past months and asked why I had not produced more recordings or written books. I explained that the economic model of Pais meant that much of my time was given to working within a church in order to provide my salary. They then inquired what it would take for me to be released to write books and devote myself full time to Pais. I replied that in order to operate independently, I would have to raise an equivalent salary I had been earning from the church. Nothing more was said.

On the drive, we learned that my planned hosts in Steamboat had an unexpected situation arise which meant it was problematic to house me. Graciously, the couple offered their basement apartment for the week.

The week was a fun week of preaching. My itinerary went well; I had a good time with the team and an interview with a school we were told would never allow us to step foot on its campus. Early in the week, my hosts asked if we could have dinner together sometime during the week, and, of course, I agreed.

And then, the thing you only ever read about in books happened...

They dropped the bomb.

They offered to *fund* my *full* salary.

For about ten minutes I was in a daze, not fully understanding what they were saying. At first I thought perhaps they were thinking about helping *towards* my salary. Then it gradually dawned on me they weren't just airing some idea but had already made the decision. This couple, who had been attempting to go overseas as missionaries thinking it was God's will, yet having the door closed over and over, had been led instead to support me financially. I had sat down to dinner with not a single cent previously pledged towards this new venture and walked away from dessert with the whole amount.

You have to understand, nothing like this had ever happened to me before. The biggest gift I had received previously was the grant I mentioned of around £4000,[107] but that was fifteen years ago. This was provision in a whole new league. My new patrons were also pioneers. In the last fifteen years, I have had the pleasure of meeting and getting to know some wealthy people, but this couple would not have fallen into that category. What they were giving was much more than a tithe. It was a sacrifice to the Lord which would undoubtedly cause a serious dent in their family's finances.

The lesson?

God will provide in many different ways, none of which you will expect.

talmidim

The message of this chapter is a forewarning that you *will* be tempted to compromise. Finance and status are two temptations that try to keep us from going the extra mile. A third is people.

Remember, the phrase 'A Pioneer' is an oxymoron.

It takes only one person to change the world but that one person cannot do it alone.

And therein lies the paradox: God gives revelation to an individual, but for the vision to be realized, it must be imparted to a community who will join the movement.

When the apostle Paul was pioneering this new faith, he travelled where common sense, strategy, and experience led him. One day, however, God called him through a dream to Macedonia. Now look carefully at the words recorded by those journeying with him.

> *After Paul had seen the vision, we got ready at once to leave for Macedonia, concluding that God had called us to preach the gospel to them.*[108]

Do you notice the mindset of those with him?

Let me ask you a question.

Who actually saw the vision?

Only Paul.

Because God had called Paul, his travel companions concluded that He had called them as well. Such has to be the tightness of a group of people to change the world.

Remember what we learned earlier about talmidim. Students wanted to *know* what their rabbi knew. Talmidim wanted to *be* who their rabbi was.

Students maintain the kingdom. Talmidim advance it.

Students have their own lives, and they remain very separate and distinct. They do their own thing, but seek their rabbi's knowledge in order to make their own lives better. The lives of the talmidim, however, were intricately woven together with the life of the rabbi.

Talmidim made their relationships with their rabbi of foremost importance. This relationship was seen as higher than that of a son with his own father. The Jews had a saying: *Although a man's father brings him into the world, his master [rabbi] brings him into the world to come,*[109] therefore the relationship between a rabbi and a disciple took precedence over the one with his father and his own flesh and blood.

According to Jewish oral law, if a disciple's father and teacher were taken captive, the disciple must first ransom his teacher and then only afterwards, his father.[110]

That's harsh. Harsher still, was something Jesus said:

> *If anyone comes to me and does not hate his father and mother, his wife and children, his brothers and sisters—yes, even his own life—he cannot be my disciple.*[111]

The way in which Jesus employs the word *hate* comes from a Hebrew idiom which uses extreme comparisons to emphasize a point. In other words, Jesus did not use *hate* in a literal sense. Rather, a man's love for his rabbi should be so strong that it makes his feelings toward his father look like hate in comparison.

Jesus also said:

> *Anyone who loves his father or mother more than me is not worthy of me; anyone who loves his son or daughter more than me is not worthy of me; and anyone who does not take his cross and follow me is not worthy of me.*[112]

Why?

It is not so much the act of *witness* which advances the Kingdom of God, but rather the act of *with-ness*.

Pioneers can't compromise by allowing just anyone to embark on the journey with them. Even of those individuals we would most dearly like to join us in the journey, we have to ask the awkward questions.

It was not uncommon for students to leave Jesus. Even after an inspiring sermon, large groups simply walked away.[113]

You as a pioneer will face the same pressure Jesus did. People are vital to your vision, and great people are like gold dust. But you must resist the pressure to conform and essentially franchise your vision to anyone who just wants to know what you know and do what you do.

You need people who want to *be* who you *are*.

THE LINE AND THE DOT ∴ STAGE THREE

questions for the pioneer

1. If compromise is *"a settlement of a dispute in which two or more sides agree to accept less than they originally wanted"* are you being tempted to settle for less than you originally wanted?

2. Write a list of strange incidents where what you needed has been provided for. What does this list teach you?

3. You have one million dollars. You want to invest it where it will do the most good. Would you invest it in you?

STAGE FOUR ✧ REPRODUCTION

STAGE FOUR

REPRODUCTION | MY STORY

spark

A seed is just another version of a spark.

My dream is to spark a global movement.

It is my hope that one day a typical church leader will walk into a conference or gathering of colleagues and be asked a new kind of question. Usually most ministers meet and greet, and after less than five minutes of small talk, the inevitable questions drop from their lips:

> *How big is your church?*
> *How many attend?*
> *Do you do home groups? Small groups?*
> *Are they cell-based or G-12?*

These and several other tools are used for gathering information and ideas. My hope is that a different question will drop from people's lips:

> *How do you serve your local schools?*

Or much more importantly:

> *What creative ways are you using to impact the young people in your community?*

I live for a future in which churches no longer see youth ministry as simply catering to the needs of the young people and parents within the congregation. A day instead will come where they pioneer new methods to embrace the youth in the community they are responsible for.

I will probably die before that happens.

My hope, however, is that my eyes might see the first signs of a shift in that direction on a worldwide scale.

As a pioneer, I only had a seed to work with. This seed contained the vision. A seed is not yet the full plant; it does not look like the plant, taste like the plant, or smell like the plant. And yet it contains within it almost everything the plant will eventually require. It carries its DNA. It carries its life source.

[In the third book of the trilogy, *The Seed and the Cloud,* we will look into this more deeply.]

After almost two decades of pioneering Pais, I have gone from seeing the first shoots to the growth of a tree whose branches have spread wider than I ever imagined they would.

A long time ago, a Christian leader approached me with what he said was a word for me from God:

> *Paul, I think God sees you like a tree whose roots, rather than going very deep, have stretched very wide. You have and you will continue to find new sources of nutrition and feed in places outside of the people in your network. This will lead to a tree with wide branches that numerous and many types of birds will find shelter in.*

I guess this is beginning to come true. When I was working on my own in seventeen different schools, I taught around 10,000 students per year and connected only a few of them to a Christian community. At this point in time, Pais has completely lost track of how many young people we have shared our message with, but a conservative estimate would be around 1.5 million students, 99.5% of them being reached in public schools. We have integrated, at the very least, several thousand into their local churches.

Impact comes not from addition but multiplication.

And where does multiplication come from?

Reproduction.

> *I tell you the truth, unless a kernel of wheat falls to the ground and dies, it remains only a single seed. But if it dies, it produces many seeds.*[114]

arrows[1]

It has been said that peace always follows war. Sometimes life seems to be a series of battles. We cannot build in wartime because war consumes our resources, our strategies, and our energy. However, in the peace that is eventually won, great things can be built, and it can be done at a much faster pace.

David fought and won peace, and with that peace, Solomon built a golden age. I want to encourage you that in this fourth stage of pioneering, your dreams can come true and, more importantly, so can the dreams of others.

It is difficult to put into words the feelings I experience when I read a Pais ministry status update on facebook about students in Africa or Asia or Europe who have come to know Christ for the first time.

It is hard to encapsulate the sense of understanding that gradually dawns on you when you realize that not only were their young lives changed, but you just indirectly catapulted your spiritual spark into their children whose destiny has now also been impacted. That young person's child will now grow up in a Christian family that knows God, with spiritual brothers and sisters they would have never known before.

It is impossible to communicate the mixed feelings of thankfulness and nostalgia when I think of the early Pais leaders—Adam, Andy, Rachel, Tina, Steve, Beccy, Mark, and so many others—who worked together so hard with so much sacrifice, for a dream that was only a fraction of what God had in mind.

One day an American friend was doing what only Americans do best: analyzing the statistics. He turned to me and said, "Paul, do you realize that last year in GB alone we connected and shared our message with more than a quarter of a million young people in assemblies and lessons?"

Houses can be robbed, cars can be wrecked, bodies can fall apart, stock markets can crash, but those words and that joy will never rust, be eaten away, broken into, or stolen.

I am inspired by this truth and the song that encapsulates it, written almost 3,000 years ago.

Psalm 127 speaks to me on two levels.

> *Unless the Lord builds the house, its builders labor in vain.*
> *Unless the Lord watches over the city, the watchmen stand guard in vain.*
>
> *In vain you rise early and stay up late, toiling for food to eat— for he grants sleep to those he loves.*[115]

Lynn and I have spent the last 21 years of marriage with a kind of role reversal relationship. She is the practical one. If a shelf needs fixing, she will mend it or if a wall needs painting, she's onto it. Any handyman job and she's the woman of choice. When we walk around Home Depot, Lynn is the one inspecting the multi-drills, and I'm the one who points to a can of paint and makes comments like: "Oooh, salmon pink would be nice for the bathroom!"

I totally understand 'builders laboring in vain' to construct a house. Who wants to spend a lot of hard work and see something fall apart rather than grow and grow?

I also realize, however, that the second half of the Psalm provides the solution to the problem of the first half:

> *Sons are a heritage from the Lord, children a reward from him.*
> *Like arrows in the hands of a warrior are sons born in one's youth.*
> *Blessed is the man whose quiver is full of them.*
> *They will not be put to shame when they contend with their enemies in the gate.*[116]

The young people we engage with are without doubt like these arrows. I can spiritually fight face-to-face with one opponent but I can shoot these arrows the extra mile. We can fire them into distant battles in factories, offices, networks, societies, cultures, and nations that we will never set foot in.

Students are like arrows we shoot into a future we cannot enter.

Pais is about guerilla warfare. It is grass roots with no clear centralized headquarters; it is therefore very hard for our enemy to kill off. Things are now happening through Pais that I will never even hear of.

I am no longer in control. And that is a very healthy thing.

Pioneer, I promise you that you will not labor in vain if you are able to multiply yourself and reproduce that seed in young people around you. Joy does not come in a moment. It is the result of a process.

Recently I heard a phenomenal young woman speak who is now blushing as she types this because she is also the one who takes down my dictation. As Sebrina inspired us to dig deeper into God's Word, she shared an illustration from Donald Miller's book, *A Million Miles in a Thousand Years*. She simply told us this:

> There was an easy way to get to the top of the Inca trail that took only six hours, but the travelers decided to take the four day route. Why? Because the more painful the journey, the more you appreciate the summit.

Simple but true.

stories

I have stories.

They are numerous enough to mention.

But my stories have stories.

And they are too numerous to mention.

My stories are the people I have worked with—the people who have labored with me over the years. I read them and learn from them. They are like encyclopedias to me. They give me reference points, advice, encouragement.

Their stories inspire me. They show how the journey of a pioneer eventually evolves into something that reproduces itself, by first influencing others and then being adopted and adapted by them.

REPRODUCTION || MY STORY

chris c's story [usa]

My fiancée and I had both served on Pais in England and the USA for three years when we looked towards a new challenge: to make missionaries in a children's academy and orphanage in Granbury, Texas. The nature of the environment meant we would authentically "do life" with these young men and women, living in dorms above theirs, eating meals in the large dining hall, helping them in the on-campus school, watching TV with them and hanging out on hallway floors talking late into the night, seven days a week. The lives of those on our team would truly be transparent.

When we arrived, the students described Christianity as dull, routine, and pointless. Many were from problematic backgrounds, difficult families, or had been in trouble with the police. For some, this was their last chance. Our team each mentored ten students one-on-one on a bi-weekly basis, equipping them to serve and live missionally on the campus. We helped with the youth service on Sunday nights, supported students, and shared our faith both through our words and our actions. Over the year, students began truly worshipping, praying, leading devotions, and becoming actively involved members of the on-site church rather than mere spectators. They took ownership of the media and drama within the service, formed a student-led worship band, and reached out to the younger elementary aged children by building relationships, teaching them life principles, and developing their character.

One young man in particular had natural leadership ability but used it abusively, influencing other students to be disrespectful, hateful, and persistently against the changes we sought to bring. The time I spent with this student was lengthy and costly to my social life, but not a minute was wasted. I watched him become the one to bring calm rather than calamity, asking challenging questions and teaching truth to those he lived with. He became the quarterback of the varsity football team and was the first to bend his knee in prayer on the field, leading the team to follow suit. He was and is an inspiration to me as I watched him learn to live life to the fullest and help his house buddies do the same.

Currently, my wife and I are helping Pais in its partnership with an American mega church of over 8,000 people. The church's vision was shifting from an attractional model to a community-based strategy.[117] As part of this, we grew from having one team our first year here to five teams the second year, and eventually we hope to multiply until there are teams in every high school in the city. Our teams influence students through teaching lessons—we were able to teach about Godly relationships to the entire freshman class of one school. We have begun working with a government initiative to keep students in schools and away from teenage pregnancy. As part of a Christmas project, 33 students decided that they wanted to counteract the pagan media-driven holiday it had become, and distributed 400 personalised, handwritten cards to specific individuals they knew who did not know Christ, writing encouraging words of peace, joy, and truth. The ministry opportunities still involve their own rounds of wrestling and perseverance, but it is exciting to know that we are producing missionaries all across the city. Students are graduating high school and joining us full time, some have become God Bringers, bringing friends to church, and others have started prayer groups and new on-campus academies, serving students and faculty in their schools.

Two words come to mind when I think of Chris: one is faithfulness and the other, perhaps even more fitting, is tenacity. Chris is a fighter. He's extremely keen to see the Kingdom of God advanced in and through him. Along with his wife Emma, they bring a true faithfulness to the vision of Pais and are a couple we can always rely on to pioneer and build anywhere we have sent them. If every Pais apprentice had the stubbornness and determination of Chris, the world would be a better place.

rachel s' story [usa]

It is an understatement to say that I am not a small town girl: I grew up near Washington, DC, attended Bible college in California, and served my first Pais year in Arlington, Texas. When I began team leading in the South Routt area of Colorado, working in three towns with a combined population of just 3000, I remember thinking, "God, what have you gotten me into? How could you send a crazy loud mouth 'Valley girl' to the middle of nowhere?!"

Coming from a vibrant ministry in the metroplex, my first week at my new youth group stunned me. There were only ten students, and compared to my first year on Pais, they seemed, at least to me, unenthusiastic and uninspired. I knew the church had a real love for their young people, and I realized instantly why God had sent me. I prayed, "If I am here for a year, things will change!"

After two weeks of watching the youth group stagnate, my team and I were asked to take over. We embraced this opportunity, making flyers for the youth group and posting them on every single door in town, handing them out at a Labor Day parade and throwing ourselves into the life of the community. Our first night 'in charge,' 30 students attended. The next week, more came. In three short months, we saw 80 students come along.

To serve within the local schools in any capacity, we had to get substitute teacher licenses, which proved to be a lengthy process. Not wanting to waste time, we brainstormed about ways to make an impact outside of the usual lunch clubs and classes. We attended every single school sporting event we could, building deep relationships and openly speaking about our events, youth group, and God. We worked concession stands at games and chaperoned a dance. When we found out most students hung out after school at local parks, we met them there. We went on prayer walks through the town asking God to move in powerful ways.

We are seeing real change happen in this place. We minister to students with drug problems and alcoholic parents that were previously deemed unreachable. One student told us that it was assumed that everyone in the town was considered bad, but the Pais team had changed that. Three students I mentor started a Christian club at their school. Our small community is now full of students hungry for God's truth. A light really has been shone in a dark place.

My wife Lynn is fascinated by Rachel. When I met Rachel, I was told in no uncertain words that she was the epitome of a 'Valley girl'. At the time I didn't really understand what that was; I certainly do now. Most young people are enthusiastic, but there is a difference between enthusiasm for what you do and passion for those you work with. Rachel is a passionate person; she is a pioneer. In her first year on Pais, I possibly challenged and rebuked her more than the average apprentice, but if I were to choose twelve disciples from the last couple of years, she would be my Peter. Rachel walks on water. Some might say that's because she doesn't have the common sense to know she might drown, but I think it's because she can see more clearly than most what she's walking towards.

tony's story [usa]

In all honesty, when I first heard Paul speak about Pais while he was recruiting apprentices in the US, I thought he was full of it. After many years as a youth pastor in the states, my paradigm could not accept that ministry in public school was even possible much less able to be accomplished like Paul described in his session. However, one of my graduating students was really interested in joining the project.

A couple of days later, with my student's desire firmly placed in my mind, I took Paul out to lunch and we discussed Pais and ministry in American public schools. Somewhere in the conversation, Paul asked me, "Tony, do you believe Pais could work in America?" Frankly, the question caught me off guard. On one hand, the separation of church and state as it applied to public schools had really heated up in legal circles and court cases. On the other hand, God is God and He can do whatever He wants. After a very pregnant pause, I responded, explaining that I didn't know how it could be done, but if God was for it, who could be against it? So, yes, Pais could work in America.

A few months later, I went to England to determine if Pais was a legitimate, safe, and healthy organization for my graduating students to serve with. If I am honest, I expected to find a ministry that was sort of doing what Paul had described but lacking the robustness he had articulated. After spending time with Paul and his family and being embedded with a schools team for a week, I left England shocked that not only was Pais executing what Paul had said, but in actuality, he had been very humble and understated regarding Pais and its accomplishments in England. My paradigm was blown, my passion for uniting students of faith in schools rekindled, and I was hooked. I soon found myself facilitating the first team in the USA, and gradually, after building local networks and bringing slow but steady growth, I became the National Director for Pais:USA.

The first few years were quite a journey: partnering with churches, recruiting apprentices, finding funding, building relationships with school administrators and teachers, and most importantly, finding how Pais could operate in public schools without violating federal law and placing schools in compromising situations. We were not, of course, the first youth organization to go onto a school campus, but it *was the manner in which Pais served and connected with the school that surprised even me. We were doing more than simply visiting our own youth group students at lunch times. Openings to teach lessons and mentor students began to happen across the board. What became apparent was that the principles and professionalism of Pais, rather than the particular programs, were winning the trust of the schools' faculty.*

After a slow start, Pais:USA gained credibility and has become a ministry that even some larger and more influential churches are adopting. I'm happy to say I've been able to pass on a ministry that has proven itself to work. I am now assisting Paul with training our long term leaders by establishing a three-year apprenticeship model, and I take great joy in watching Pais:USA flourish in the country that I love.

I doubt if there would be a Pais Project in the USA if it had not been for a random meeting with Tony. Until our discussion, I could find no one who would take a risk, pouring time and effort into the hope of bringing our vision to America. Tony believed in me and also in *it*, and for this I am truly grateful. It is always a pleasure to work with Tony. Watching him gently hand over something that was growing in order to help us in new areas has been both an inspiration and a lesson to many of us within the movement.

nic and sarah's story [thailand]

God spoke to Sarah about being a missionary when she was four, although she was very disabled at that point. Born with Osteogensis Imperfecta (Brittle Bone Disease), Sarah's bones would break far more easily than most people's and she had difficultly even walking. She broke her finger when she opened a half-empty bottle of coke and her hand slipped. Excess bone growth around the ear drum built up over time which stopped the ear drum vibrating and caused gradual deafness. At age 10, after doctors told her they could do nothing more, her brother prayed for her and for the first time, she was able to live without a wheelchair. At age 16, after a failed operation on her ears, she went to a youth conference desperate for healing. During the worship, she heard a pop within her ears and could hear— tests confirmed that her hearing was completely restored.

As fulfillment of the calling to the mission field, the opportunity arose for Sarah and I to pioneer Pais in Asia after having served three years on the Pais national directorship in Great Britain. During early conversations with other missionaries and organizations in Asia, it became apparent that we, as individuals and as Pais, did not fit any of the old categories they had. We began to realize just how unique Pais was and became more excited about seeing young people reached through its ministry. Taking the vision to a new and non-Western culture would mean being flexible and adaptable, but also holding onto the fundamentals of what makes Pais Pais. Many Christians told us we could not go into student communities as Christians, insistent that the Buddhist nation would reject us. Within two weeks of networking meetings, five different opportunities opened up, fully understanding the faith of us and our volunteers. We continued to reach into otherwise inaccessible student communities on behalf of our church. Our reputation within schools grew and we held a prominent role supporting them. In our second year, our team regularly saw over 125 young people 2-3 times a week. We were so excited when the first students began attending the local youth group. Young people were integrated into our initiatives such as M4, which we called i⁺.

We found that we didn't have to change the principles of Pais strategy which was an encouragement to us. Eventually however, a problem we did not foresee began to emerge. Over a period of time, and very gradually, our platform, networking opportunities, and finances were taken away from us. Initially we struggled to understand the reason for this, but now feel it may have been the success of what was happening making others feel uncomfortable, and perhaps even threatened. This began to frustrate us, even affecting our hearts and minds. At times we began to question if we had done something wrong.

During this time, our teams were seeing 250 young people a week, in eight different communities. High schools and universities were contacting us about running semester long workshops but we were having to turn down schools work due to a lack of man power. The city Major even commented on Pais' contribution to the poorer urban schools and offered financial support for the team. As we sought to expand into Asian nations, many spoke to us about how unique Pais was in its ethos. They too, it seemed, although at first skeptical about the vision, wanted to see it happen where they were.

One thing I love about Nic and Sarah has been their breaking away from the line. There is definitely a distance between them and the traditional way of making a communal impact. Even in the new culture which they embraced and immersed themselves in, to them the common methods had become a dot. When first arriving in Thailand, they did not have Christian networks to help provide financial resources. Instead, after seeing their presentations, a local hotel manager contacted them, and so began a new venture for Pais whereby our teams began training resort staff in the tourist parts of Phuket. This tsunami stricken territory was being regenerated not simply with new hotel buildings, but elements of Pais DNA were injected into programs and care was provided for the tourists' children. Nic and Sarah's story is in some ways tinged with sadness though, because as they shared, their resources dried up to such a degree that the teams had to leave their part of Thailand. Their legacy, however, is that we are now inundated with networks and contacts throughout the Pacific Rim who saw what they did and are speaking to us about Pais coming to their cities.

beccy's story [gb]

It was my second year on Pais, team leading in Croydon, England. Throughout the year, my team would take a break from our heavy schedule in schools and have prayer and fasting days. On one particular day, I felt God instruct us to challenge the students we worked with in our biggest lunchtime club at the local Church of England school. The challenge was simply: to become followers of God. We had previously taught on all manner of theological issues, some of which were quite deep, so it seemed like a step back to challenge them in this rudimentary way, but when I brought the idea to my team, they loved it. I remained fearful, and constantly prayed, "God please help us," knowing that it would fall flat without His aid.

The day arrived and we went through our presentation of teaching through personal stories mixed with music. The final section ended. I announced that we were finished and all were free to leave, but if they wanted to make the decision to become a Christian, they could stay and we would pray with them. No one moved. I repeated it again, assuming they hadn't understood. Four students got up and left. Everyone else stayed seated. I couldn't believe it. A hushed silence fell upon the room as they all waited attentively. That day, 54 young people responded and took up the challenge. On Pais, at the end of our sessions, we always had some form of follow-up or defining moment, but on this day we simply didn't have enough materials and were not prepared for such a high number.

The next day we were in a rough and troubled school where we didn't know any Christian students. Though we had another presentation planned, I felt God tell me to do the same one again. I was unsure, but so elated from what had happened the day before that I rearranged it all. Twenty students responded to the challenge. In the following weeks, they brought friends to the club. We even recreated church services at lunchtime so they could see what church was like. Prayers were answered. A parent was healed. I was encouraged and glad that I had learned to step away from the system and be led by God's Spirit.

Beccy's story is really encouraging to me because perhaps the greatest joy for a pioneer is to see one's DNA and spirit passed on rather than just the programs or systems. I loved how Beccy decided not to rely on routines or brainstorm ideas, but how she gave space for revelation. Beccy went on to become my Personal Assistant, partly because of her organizational skills and bubbly personality, but mainly because whenever she represented me, I was confident that she would be able to convey the heart and mind of our vision. It was guaranteed that when people met Beccy they would think higher of me and Pais.

arrows[2]

An ancient king named Jehoash was facing incredible odds. He was not the most spiritual of men, but he knew he needed God. So he went to the one man who represented to him the King of Kings: a man named Elisha.

> *Now Elisha was suffering from the illness from which he died. Jehoash king of Israel went down to see him and wept over him. "My father! My father!" he cried. "The chariots and horsemen of Israel!"*[118]

What was Jehoash saying here?

We have to understand the ancient Hebrews had a language that described things by their function. Jehoash is stating that Elisha is the only hope of his nation. The king was facing Aram with a small police force. He'd inherited only ten chariots, fifty horsemen, and about ten thousand soldiers. In 857 BC, his opponent Ahab destroyed ten times as many foot soldiers in one day. Jehoash recognized that Elisha represented Israel's only real military force...God.

> Elisha said, "Get a bow and some arrows," and he did so. "Take the bow in your hands," he said to the king of Israel. When he had taken it, Elisha put his hands on the king's hands.
>
> "Open the east window," he said, and he opened it. "Shoot!" Elisha said, and he shot. "The Lord's arrow of victory, the arrow of victory over Aram!" Elisha declared. "You will completely destroy the Arameans at Aphek."[119]

Why shoot an arrow? This was an ancient tradition of declaring war. If you felt you had been done an injustice, you could go the edge of the territory of your prospective enemy and shoot an arrow into their land, stating your grievance. The practice said that thirty days were given for a peaceable settlement. If there were no resolution, war would follow.[120]

You can tell when a man of God intervenes or enters your life; the intervention changes your world from a position of defense to an attitude of attack.

> Then he said, "Take the arrows," and the king took them. Elisha told him, "Strike the ground." He struck it three times and stopped. The man of God was angry with him and said, "You should have struck the ground five or six times; then you would have defeated Aram and completely destroyed it. But now you will defeat it only three times."[121]

What was going through Jehoash's mind when he struck the ground only three times?

Ponder that for a moment.

Why do you think he did it?

Apathy?

Embarrassment?

A lack of understanding?

Something else?

The answer that comes to your mind may not be what was in the heart of Jehoash, but may give you insight into what is in your heart and why at times it is possible that you will not go the extra mile.

I love the connection of the song about arrows and the story of arrows.

Do you see it?

questions for the pioneer

1. Will your vision be completed before you die?
2. Can your vision be reproduced? Is it transferable? Is it repeatable?
3. What brings you the most delight—when you succeed or when those around you succeed?

STAGE FOUR

REPRODUCTION | OUR STORY

tupperware

Several years ago I was watching a BBC news program. The big issue of the day was a group of young environmental activists who had spent months protesting the construction of a new highway, the A30, in a rural part of England. These activists looked like militaristic earth hippies. They had names like 'Stick' and 'Butterfly'. The one I distinctly remember was called 'Swampy'.[122] At age 22, he and his fellow eco warriors dug tunnels underground and set traps for those who might try to pull them out. Incredibly, the traps did not really hurt their pursuers but meant that the protesters themselves would be buried alive. This led to a standoff lasting the best part of a year. I often tuned in to find out who was winning this battle of wills, but one particular time a side-line story caught my attention. I watched as a small group of local middle-aged, extremely conservative English ladies were filmed during their daily lunchtime routine. These concerned surrogate mothers and grandmothers, dressed in their rural middle class attire, carried Thermos flasks and neatly packed Tupperware boxes to distribute to their new friends Swampy and Co. I listened intently as the interviewer asked a selection of ladies why they were so committed to looking after a group of smelly, rebellious, and unkempt young people. Their answer fascinated me. It turned out that although they did not agree with Swampy's methods or politics, they had been swayed by his commitment and passion. They shared how they had been previously ignorant of environmental issues but now had begun to campaign in their own conservative way about the treatment of the surrounding area.

It takes an extreme to influence the mainstream.

Extremists are on one side of the pendulum, and the mainstream may be on the opposite side. The passion of extremists and their commitment to go the extra mile swings the mainstream pendulum towards them. Those in the mainstream will rarely become as fanatical or as single-minded about that one particular issue, but they will become more than simply aware; they will be shifted to the middle ground.

Pais is the extreme that I believe will influence the mainstream. Our single-mindedness is a spark and a seed. It is not, of course, our intention that everybody should become a schools and youth worker or even that every church should adopt a Pais team. Our hope instead is that, through complete commitment to our schools, other 'Swampy's will cause the mainstream church to take seriously the opportunity, potential, and responsibility to impact the youth of their community rather than just the youth of their church.

acts

The fourth stage of pioneering is reproduction.

> *And anyone who does not take his cross and follow me is not worthy of me. Whoever finds his life will lose it, and whoever loses his life for my sake will find it.*[123]

Once you have had a revelation and passed the test of being a loner, then those who did not believe in *it* will become threatened by the revolution that you are causing. In the third stage, you resist the temptation to conform and compromise in order to receive the resources so desperately needed, and as the years go by, the new path you have created becomes so well worn that others begin to walk down it. You have entered the fourth stage. What was the alternative path is now the new highway. It becomes wider and wider.

However, a new danger presents itself. The dot becomes the new line.

Jesus did not come to die upon the cross. He came to reproduce Himself. The cross was simply part of the process of creating a new path. For Jesus to see the Kingdom come, He would need others to copy His example, to pick up their own crosses and to walk down a similar path.

And that is exactly what happened.

> *Everyone was filled with awe, and many wonders and miraculous signs were done by the apostles. All the believers were together and had everything in common. Selling their possessions and goods, they gave to anyone as he had need. Every day they continued to meet together in the temple courts. They broke bread in their homes and ate together with glad and sincere*

> hearts, praising God and enjoying the favor of all the people. And the Lord added to their number daily those who were being saved.[124]

Jesus had successfully begun to turn His world upside down. Slaves would eat alongside masters. The rich would feed the poor. The weak would become strong.

Jesus uncovered what all other pioneers will discover. In the stage of revelation you will have to sacrifice, but in the season of reproduction, many others will sacrifice because they now finally see *it*.

Joanna, the wife of Cuza who was one of King Herod's chief administrators, became one of Jesus' financial supporters. Other wealthy sponsors also invested in Jesus' mission. Susanna and later Joseph of Arimathea came out of the woodwork and got onboard with the most comprehensive global plan of all time.

This fourth stage of pioneering is exciting not simply because people give; it is an adventure all in itself as it produces new pioneers.

> *I tell you the truth, anyone who has faith in me will do what I have been doing. He will do even greater things than these...*[125]

It is estimated there are around 2.1 billion Christians in the world.[126]

That's one third of the world's population.

What if one third of the world's population did even greater things than Jesus?

Is the greatest sin of the church not, in fact, what we think it is?

toms

Within the youth ministry that Pais repurposed in Fort Worth, Texas, my team and I found that the most productive teachings were those which stretched the students. With this in mind, we spent eight weeks looking at the four stages of Kingdom Pioneering. We challenged them that God was looking for people who would do things differently. And then, a little more controversially, we took them through the four stages, looking behind the scenes of Christianity and the politics they would face if they chose to swim against the flow. In that series, the current we challenged them to swim against was not that of secular culture but of line-dwelling Christian culture.

In the first sermon, I used the example of TOMS Shoes. This *for-profit* company sells a certain type of shoe, and for each pair purchased, they give another pair to a child in a developing country who has no shoes. It was especially relevant as members of the CEO's family had previously attended the church. On that first week, I asked them to raise their hands if they had heard of the brand. Less than 5% had. I showed them the documentary of the founder as he told the story of his company and what he hoped to achieve. The video showed the TOMS team fitting masses of barefoot, poverty-stricken children with their first pair of shoes, bringing tears to the eyes of many students. After the video finished, I asked them what they thought his big vision was. Many of them said to give free shoes away to those who could not afford them.

I told them they were wrong.

His vision, I said, is to change the way businesses think and to influence other CEO's to adopt a policy of two for one. They wanted to create an economic model whereby for every unit of product purchased, a free unit could be given to someone in need.

It is a brilliant concept, and it could apply to absolutely anything: food, energy, medicine, housing, technology, transportation, communication. The possibilities are endless.

Nobody in that room had heard him say it, nobody got it, nobody realized it, but if this pioneer fulfilled his dream, then giving away mere millions of free shoes would be a drop in the ocean. It could fade into insignificance when compared to what it inspired others to do. Its significance would not be in its direct influence but in its *indirect* influence.

It would be the extreme that influenced the mainstream.

I remember sharing this thought with them and telling them the stages that he would probably go through if he were to be a true pioneer and see a new path opened up. I explained that you do not have to travel the world in order to change it; you have to change your world and then the rest of the globe would come to see what you had done and how they could copy it. I shared that one day I believed TOMS Shoes would be courted by many other much bigger corporations.

The week leading up to the last sermon in the series, the one on Reproduction, I heard a shout from my family.

> "Dad! Come and look at the TV!"

I ran from my study to catch the end of a brand new AT&T commercial in which Blake Mycoskie, TOMS Shoes founder and Chief Shoe Giver, shared his vision and his new shiny phone. The timing was perfect.

It seems to me though that nobody wants to be the pioneer.

Too many would rather wait for someone else to develop a proven program or structure that they can adopt. We travel far and wide to the latest conferences, hoping to find a surefire way to increase our organization or church's growth. We want someone else to face the risks and take the chances for us.

It is safer. It is more secure. It is more financially stable.

...The love of money is the root of all evil.

But what is evil?

het

According to the Jewish encyclopedia, there are various categories of sin. The three most commonly discussed can teach us something about the line and the dot.

First is *pesha*. This category is the worst type of sin. The meaning of *pesha* is to commit a rebellious act. But it is more than a simple act of rebellion; there is a deeper connotation, a deeper sense of what sin is.

Sin is not a breaking of *rules* but a breaking of *relationship*.

Pesha implies a willful departure from the authority of the one who gave the command. In other words, *pesha* usually denotes a deliberate rebellion against our Father by the act of breaking His law.

The second category of sin is *awon*, or what you might call the middle ground. The meaning of *awon* is to commit a breach of a commandment. Its meaning "to breach" reminds me of a huge dam holding back millions of gallons of water. A breach in the dam, no matter how small, will allow water to squirt through. My understanding is that *awon* is the kind of sin you commit with full knowledge even though you consider yourself a follower of God. It is in this middle ground that many of us go round and round in circles. We spend much of our time wrestling with the same kinds of sin.

The third category is *het*. The meaning of *het* is to 'omit' rather than 'commit'. More specifically, *het* means a shortcoming, a misstep. It is the category of line-dwelling whereby we sin as a result of not going the extra mile.

Is *het* our biggest adversary?

Not fulfilling, not pursuing, not going beyond ourselves?

The Jewish word for commandment is *mitzvah*. For many of us, our approach to the commandments is that we try to not break them. A Hebraic understanding focuses on fulfilling a commandment, rather than avoiding breaking one.

How might our lives be different, how might the Kingdom be advanced, if we had the attitude of many history-changers, an attitude which excitedly proclaims, "Today I got the chance to fulfill a *mitzvah*!"

To overcome the sin of *het* is to break free from the boundaries that fence us in, to go beyond the common. It might be to clean up our act and pursue holiness of heart and motives rather than just holiness in outward appearances and actions. At the other end of the line, overcoming *het* may mean to surpass the fence of common expectations. It may mean thinking of new and creative ways to show kindness rather than simply making sure you fulfill accepted neighborly traditions. Moving away from *het* is moving away from the line, and the further we move away, the smaller the line appears until we reach our goal of only seeing the dot.

Evil is always willing to compromise because it doesn't really have an ideal. The devil does not have a dream of an 'evil you'... just a 'compromised you', an 'unfulfilled you', a 'line-dwelling you'.

flop

As it has been said, everything is spiritual.

Therefore this Kingdom process infiltrates all of life. The words and story of Jesus do not simply teach us about religion, but about the dynamics of the way God orders His world. In sports, we see this process of pioneering.

Something happened in the 1960s that allowed athletes to set records in a whole new league. Dick Fosbury changed the way high jumpers competed by reinventing a whole new method of high-jumping. Totally ridiculed in the early days, Fosbury would run in an arc like motion towards his goal and then run backwards for the last few steps jumping behind himself. Although people believed in Fosbury, they did not believe in 'the flop'. However, his gold medal in the 1968 Summer Olympics changed all that. The old systems of the straddle, roll, and scissors techniques became almost obsolete. A new path had been formed in this specific sport, and now everyone who competes seriously adopts 'the flop'.

Perhaps the most obvious place we see the four stages of pioneering is in the area of business. A great example would be Anita Roddick who started her first shop sandwiched in between two funeral parlors, subsequently—and controversially—naming her business The Body Shop. She pioneered new forms of ethics and fair trade in the 1970s. Like most pioneers, she started very small. Rarely does a pioneer start with big backing or even adequate resources. Her small cosmetics store was on a back street away from the flow of walk-by customers. Roddick demonstrated one of the key distinctives of a pioneer: she totally believed in the innate qualities of her *it*. In this case, each morning she would pour a trail of her strawberry essence along the pavement to lure the customers in. Two things would almost guarantee a sale if she could get them through the doors...this pioneer's product and her passion. Roddick was tempted to compromise on many occasions, but it was her core values rather than simply her new system that she held on to, hence her statement:

> *I'd rather promote human rights...than a bubble bath.*[127]

Many tried to copy her success to which she responded, "If only they copied our principles and not just our products."[128]

Starting with a revelation, Roddick brought a new kind of ethical revolution to the malls and market places of the world. She resisted attempts to make her conform, and now The Body Shop has been reproduced all over the globe, either by herself or through the flattery of imitation. By 2004 The Body Shop had 1,980 stores worldwide, serving over 77 million customers and was voted the 28th top brand in the world and perhaps most importantly to its founder, the 2nd most trusted brand in her nation. [129]

Pioneers become the greatest influence in any facet of humankind.[130] They come from all walks of life and in every era. In the introduction to the book, I mentioned the contemporary pioneer chef Jamie Oliver. Woody Guthrie, a pioneer of the previous generation, influenced the arts.

A charismatic, unique American folk singer, Guthrie used his superb song-writing skills to do far more than make a name for himself. He demonstrated the juxtaposition of today's celebrity culture by bringing fame more to a social issue than to himself. During the days of the Great Depression in 1930's America, Guthrie wrote songs proclaiming the injustice and exploitation of poor migrant workers. The award-winning film about his life, *Bound for Glory,* reveals how record producers, agents, and star-makers pleaded with him to remove the unpopular politics from his lyrics, offering to pay him three times more if he stopped singing songs protesting social injustice. David Carradine, the actor who depicts Guthrie, shows the gut-wrenching disappointment the singer obviously felt on several occasions when he realized his values were so different from the powers that held the keys to stardom, fame, and riches.

Guthrie died with little material wealth, but his seed was planted in the hearts of many others. What he did, which at that time was so unpopular, has now become almost fashionable.

Think Geldolf. Think Live Aid. Think Bono. Think Hope for Haiti.

inspire

Some of the pioneers that have inspired me the most are those I know personally.

Carl is a pilot. That alone impresses me.

Beyond that however, Carl has a passion to see God's Kingdom impact the small rural area of the Rocky Mountains where he lives.

More specifically, Carl has a complaint. His complaint is the way many pastors are mistreated or not well cared for. His awkward question has been, "How do we care for our leaders to keep them from burning out and then dropping out?"

Rather than simply complain about the problem, he started an outreach to church leaders called En Gedi. He raised tens of thousands of dollars in order to build a log cabin in the mountains for pastors to come to free of charge. Carl pioneered this ministry to answer a need while most people never even realized there was a question. Like all pioneers, he is ahead of his time, but he is not waiting for others to catch up before he puts flesh on his ideas.

Carl and his wife Audrey also pioneered a whole new way of looking at their personal finances in order to meet this need. Their fascinating story will be told in my next book *The Cloud and the Line*.

For now, here are more stories from pioneers on Pais. Read them. Learn from them. Be inspired by them. Their stories are our stories.

rebecca's story [canada]

At age twenty-one, after completing my third year on Pais, being trained and coached as an assistant to the National Directors of Pais:GB, I took Pais home to

Canada and started the first Canadian team in Vancouver. I arrived at our partner church with $1500 to my name. The Pais:Canada bank account had the same. Three days later, the partnering church stated they would not be paying me. Needing to get another job, I walked store to store with resumés. Despite having my own apartment, I had no way to pay for rent, food, or gas. I didn't even have a hair dryer or alarm clock. My savings were evaporating before my eyes. I slept on a foam camping mattress for six weeks before a social services agency donated a bed to me. I barely paid my bills and had food donated from a program at the church that was really only for single mothers in need. My workload increased as last minute emergency health complications with the proposed team leader meant that I would have to personally lead the team, as well as establish Pais as an independent charity and work at both the church and the local gas station.

January saw one of the worst weeks of my life when one-third of Vancouver's annual rainfall poured in three days. Our car had died so I walked 30 minutes each way to my gas station job. Nothing I owned was dry and lay strewn across my apartment in a desperate attempt to dry it. Stressed and easily snapping at my team, I remember telling a friend I was becoming the worst version of myself. It was hard to be taken seriously by other churches and ministries because of our lack of experience, resources, and Canadian connections. By Easter I was lower than I have ever been, crying out to God, wondering if He was even there, desperate for Him to be merciful to me.

God was faithful and brought in the help I needed. Paul came over and got me a salaried youth pastor role at an extremely supportive church. I realize now that the year was great in so many areas. We were in eight schools, with both churches and schools loving our work. Two apprentices stayed on for the second year. Both new applicants and churches were interested in joining us, and schools wanted us for the next academic year. Towards the end of the year, we were recognized by other prominent ministries with connections. People donated money. A car was given.

As I write this, Pais is flourishing in Canada as we are a nationally recognized ministry with several well established teams in both British Columbia and Alberta and our eyes to the east of the nation in the near future. A wonderful team is around me. My dream for Pais:Canada is to resource churches in every major urban cen-

ter. From there I see these urban hubs affecting the local suburbs and eventually spreading a movement across the nation.

Looking back, I wouldn't trade that first year. I learnt so many lessons and can see how much it has helped. The quickest way to learn is the hardest as well; like a growth spurt as a teen, your legs hurt so much. Pioneering has a way of showing you a side of God you might not see unless you get yourself in over your head. I've never regretted how hard it all was to start out, as it's become a part of my story and who I am—a small child with a big God!

I could not be more proud of Rebecca even if she were my own daughter, which is sometimes how I feel towards her. When she pioneered Pais in her home nation, she was almost five years younger than I was when I founded Pais. Hundreds of people have now demonstrated the spirit of a pioneer in our organization but perhaps none have given themselves to or have grown through the sacrifice pioneering demands as much as she has. Still at a young age, Rebecca has been asked to serve on national committees of other organizations where she acts as an advocate for Pais and advises them in her capacity as the Pais:Canada National Director.

andré's story [germany]

Years ago, German schools were more or less closed to any organization that wanted to help them. Teachers saw no need for it and didn't want the involvement of others. But then the PISA, the government evaluation of schools, came out. With this and the first school shooting, which occurred in Erfurt, our nation was shocked and realized the faults in the school system. A door into schools began to open.

Before this, Ocke, who would later become the national director for Pais:Germany, had a vision. He felt Jesus say, "You will go into the school and I will act," and so he decided to learn more about partnering with the local and national education community. After initial rejection from both church and state leaders, Ocke realized he would have to start something from a grass roots level. The solution came when Ocke was handed an audio tape of a speaker sharing strategies and principles for schools outreach at a conference with several hundred youth workers. The speaker was Paul Gibbs, and the audio tape had been passed around Germany to multiple church workers, causing a buzz and generating lots of conversation. As a result, Ocke began to establish the Pais Project in Germany, starting with the most under-privileged schools in the area. The schools no one had any hopes for. The schools no one really cared about.

Over time, Ocke changed his role with Pais, and I became National Director. Before that, I was in a phase where I thought small. I believed, and it was reaffirmed by others, that I needed to simply care for myself and my family, not getting involved in too many other things. But this small mindset slowly made me depressed. There was nothing natural about me wanting to be part of something bigger, but God repeatedly talked to me about big-ness. I read the verse from Isaiah: "Enlarge the place of your tent."[131] God demanded me to dream big, think big, and act big. Destroying my imagination of possibilities, God enlarged it again and again. Pais has become the only school or youth organization that I know of, Christian or secular, with a vision to spread all over Germany and not just settle for being in one town or region.

Within seven years of Pais:Germany, we have sent out hundreds of German apprentices to serve as missionaries on Pais. This number is so high due to our government alliance. We are registered as an official organization as part of the 'Freiwilliges Soziales Jahr' (Volunteer Social Year). I always remember my first phone call to the official from the government. He insisted that it would be impossible for us to get the license for various reasons. However, I later noticed a special paragraph in the law that would enable us to qualify. After pointing this out, those I talked to saw our position and agreed to grant us the appropriate status. National service is mandatory for young men in Germany, but through this partnership, instead of doing military service, these young men are able to serve on Pais. We hope to see thousands one day serving the young people of our nation with Pais.

Churches often reach a very small part of the society; primarily, it seems we tend to reach those who are living well with a nice house and car. With our ministry, we reach people who have never seen a Christian before. The first time I was in a school, I ran a club for designing websites with seven Turkish students, and since then we have reached people in all religions, cultures, and behaviors. We endeavor to be known as excellent schools workers who serve people from all backgrounds without bias or prejudice.

The story of Pais in Germany convinces me again that passion leads to creativity. André, along with his colleague Ocke, saw what few others could see. Then André became a pioneer within a growing organization that already had developed their way of doing things. Where most national directors recruit through speaking engagements and word of mouth, André's desperation to see the need met within schools has led him to incredible creative partnerships, one being his agreement with the German government. This process now means that many German young people with a Christian faith and proven commitment to the local church are flooding onto Pais as part of their legally mandated year of civil service. André demonstrates a manifestation of a pioneering spirit...creativity. With that, he has transformed from a man who settled to a man who has become an explorer of new ideas.

rob's story [usa]

My wife Keren and I moved from England to Texas in 1996 so I could do an MA in Cross-Cultural ministry while interning at a church in Arlington, Texas. I helped within the youth ministry, later becoming the junior high pastor. After eight years, I felt the ministry was steadily becoming directionless and stagnating. I felt discouraged. Change and consistency was needed.

After hearing about Pais at a conference, our pastor, who was instantly intrigued by the ministry, began conversations with Paul Gibbs and sent me to Manchester to investigate a possible partnership. I quickly realized this would be a huge paradigm shift from what most churches were doing in the US, including ours, but instantly saw the benefits. When Pais arrived, we deliberately combined the junior and senior high school groups, so the older students could be examples and role models. This immediately caused me a huge headache as parents with whom I had long-standing relationships were confused, concerned, and even angered by this new direction. As the Pais philosophy began to permeate our ministry, things began to change. The full-time apprentices added momentum, sparking a new desire in students to reach out to their friends and peers. Two new programs introduced the themes of intergenerational community and local mission. Both instructed them in a particular skill: one, in things such as such as media, dance, sport or prayer, which was then used as a means of teaching those in the community; the other, in care and compassion, not just for their peers, but for the wider church. This programming, combined with the change in heartbeat of the ministry, saw students empowered. I felt they weren't attending events to be entertained; they came to train and be sent out. Within my heart was a genuine sense of encouragement.

Working alongside Paul was an enlightening experience. I reveled in being part of a flourishing movement, and I myself was growing as a pioneer. Then came the big ask: Paul approached Keren and myself, asking us to take over as National Directors of Pais:USA. It seemed that everything we had previously done culminated towards this appointment. Keren came with a creative heart and a desire to get on the ground alongside the teams, while I had 20+ years of ministry experience, three years of working alongside Paul, plus a deep passion to mobilize missionaries and help local churches stop the rot of losing high school graduates because they hadn't made their faith their own.

Our heart is to move Pais:USA from being regional to national. At the time of writing we have several teams in Florida, Colorado, and various parts of Texas, including five teams at a large and influential church. They are working towards a strategy that has the potential to see forty-six Pais teams, each working within a different high school to see their city changed. Our dream is to have enough apprentices for every church that desires to partner with us. There is still much to do, but I know that we are only just at the beginning of what has the possibility of seeing a generation of missionaries desperate to make missionaries.

For the majority of my time on Pais, we have taken young inexperienced people and put the spirit of a pioneer within them. As they stayed with us, we have seen them naturally grow in their gift as time and experience have molded them. In more recent years however, this process has been inverted. We are now receiving older and wiser men and women. They have competencies beyond those of our typical apprentices, and our challenge is now to inject our DNA within them. Rob and Keren are typical of this new breed and I have been very impressed with their humility. It takes something very special for a person so entrenched and comfortable in a particular way of thinking to adopt a new way of doing. I am incredibly excited about how this couple has built an amazing young team around them and have successfully taken our vision and made Pais:USA an authentic example of what we believe in.

droppings

> *"You are the salt of the earth. But if the salt loses its saltiness, how can it be made salty again? It is no longer good for anything, except to be thrown out and trampled by men."* [132]

In Jesus' day, salt was mixed with dried animal droppings in dome-shaped ovens because the chemical reaction made the animal droppings burn hotter and longer. This must have sounded strange to Jesus' hearers—they would go out of their way to avoid mixing with the unclean people of their world.

Pioneers are not escapists.

They are not simply dreamers who live in their own little world. That is a separate kind of person.

Pioneers are sent by God to *engage, involve,* and *infiltrate*.

In 2009, chef Jamie Oliver was invited to cook at the G20 summit; delegates included President Barack Obama and other world leaders. Here is a pioneer who has begun to see his vision take root and flourish.

It is my hope that this simple book encourages your vision. I hope it empowers by forewarning you of the first three stages of pioneering. I hope that you will no longer see the tests you face as a mistake or a sign of disaster, but simply elements of the process. It is my hope that you will persevere, realizing that each stage has its own rewards, but also knowing that this fourth stage means that eventually, maybe after years of back-breaking work, there will be a tipping point whereby you will change the way things are.

It is my hope that your perseverance will result in more than just your own success, and that copycat ideas will multiply your influence without the need to manage, resource, or control those reproductions.

I hope that you will see that the greatest form of flattery is imitation.

At least, that is my hope.

questions for the pioneer

1. Can you live with being seen as an extremist? What does or does not bother you about this?

2. If it takes an extreme to influence the mainstream, where would you be happy shifting the mainstream to?

3. Relating to your vision, what are the sins of *het* you have been omitting?

STAGE FOUR

REPRODUCTION | YOUR STORY

matador

There is a particular type of vine in South America known as the *matador*.[133]

Taking root at the base of a tree, the matador vine begins its vigorous climb to the top, wrapping itself around the trunk, digging into its bark, growing upwards higher and higher. But with its growth, it brings death. Sucking life from the tree, it finally reaches its goal, the top, and as it does it crowns itself with a flower.

Any of us can succumb to the same temptation.

The final test of a pioneer is that we now become 'The Man'.

As the phrase 'A Pioneer' is an oxymoron, and by this stage we will have many others working and pioneering with us, new pioneers will be seeking to take root under the shelter of our branches. Some of the most successful people in the world are some of the most insecure people in the world. Why? Because they are afraid of losing the very thing they have worked so hard to achieve. Pioneers who want to go the full course need to develop other pioneers. That means we must now be the ones who allow those with fresh revelation to grow up among us. We must be the first to believe in them and their *it*. We must not be threatened, and we must carefully and sensitively discern between coaching and controlling. We must affirm them rather than conform them.

Here's a question you might want to begin asking yourself now before you even start along your path in this Kingdom process...

What is your aim?

To be the tree that bears fruit and seeds other trees giving God the glory? Or to be the flower that sits upon the tree giving itself the glory?

It all comes down to one word, something you start with very little of but end up with a great deal of.

Authority.

trip

Some of the stranger things Jesus did only become strange when you realize what was actually going on at the time. First listen to this conversation:

> Simon Peter answered, "You are the Christ, the Son of the living God."
>
> Jesus replied, "Blessed are you, Simon son of Jonah, for this was not revealed to you by man, but by my Father in heaven. And I tell you that you are Peter, and on this rock I will build my church, and the gates of Hades will not overcome it. I will give you the keys of the kingdom of heaven; whatever you bind on earth will be bound in heaven, and whatever you loose on earth will be loosed in heaven." [134]

Jesus had just taken His disciples on a twenty-three mile field trip. Caesarea Philippi was totally out of their way, so they were not merely passing by. This was a purposeful visit to what must have been an abhorrent place. The town stands upon a large rock, at the foot of which is the temple where the goat god Pan was worshiped. Jesus took His young disciples there, most of whom were teenagers. This was the locale for all kinds of terrible practices. Sexual perversion of the worst type involving animals went on here. Who knows what these young boys saw? So why did Jesus instigate this bizarre excursion? Rabbis taught within situation. They loved to speak about gardens within gardens, about lilies and fields among lilies and fields, and here in this case, Jesus draws their attention to a place where a spring bubbled up from underground. The pagans all around them believed this was the entrance to the gods of the underworld.

Or as they called it...the Gates of Hades.

He then tells them He will give them the keys to the Kingdom of Heaven, promising that whatever they bind will be bound and whatever they loosen will be loosened. More recently through historians such as Ray Van Der Laan,[135] this promise has brought a great understanding of Jesus' intention for His disciples. We now recognize that a rabbi would interpret the law and come up with a set of things he would permit his disciples to do alongside things he would forbid them to do. To loosen was to permit; to bind was to forbid.

Most preaching on this passage is significant but superficial. It concentrates on Peter's recognition of who Jesus was—hugely important, but merely a fraction of the whole dynamic.

Jesus takes along His disciples, the ones He has chosen because one day they can be like Him. After months of explaining His vision, His new world called the Kingdom of Heaven, He tells them it will be built on people such as the ones they are now looking at with wide eyes, butterflies, and sickening stomachs.

And then He delivers the shock and awe.

He commissions them with His authority, essentially telling them that they will become the ones who have to decipher the law and His principles in order to structure this new community that demonstrates His Kingdom.

Think about this. Jesus creates a new path. His disciples are called *followers* of the Way. But Jesus Himself will soon be no longer physically present. Soon after the moment of His crowning glory, the Resurrection, He will leave. Then, this group of young men will be responsible to shape His legacy and the community He leaves behind.

Think about this also. We know of only one disciple who was definitely no longer a teenager. This was Peter. He was the only one we can be certain had to pay the temple tax required of men over the age of twenty. Some say that the smallest of Jesus' disciples could have been as young as nine. It seems most, if not all, would have been around fourteen to twenty.

Finally, think about this. How many youth pastors do you know who would be allowed to take a group of teenage boys to a place like Caesarea Philippi?

We want to be where Jesus is, but we do not want to walk the path on which He trod to get there.

And we certainly do not want our children to do so!

tomatoes

As one leadership guru teaches, the sign of a great leader is not how much power you have, but how much you have empowered those around you.[136]

Remember the author of Hebrews, the passage we started with:

> *Do you see what this means—all these pioneers who blazed the way, all these veterans cheering us on? It means we'd better get on with it. Strip down, start running—and never quit! No extra spiritual fat, no parasitic sins. Keep your eyes on Jesus, who both began and finished this race we're in. Study how he did it.*[137]

Study how He did it.

The fact is…He did it.

What if Jesus had only made it to the third stage of pioneering, if He had convinced people His way was right but had never given His authority away? Where would our faith be now? Where would be the greatest invention of all time, the Church, be?

One of the old heroes of the Christian faith in the UK was a guy called Donald Gee. The story goes that as a child growing up in London, he once tried to grow a tomato plant. At that time, the air of England's capital was deeply polluted. Smog blocked out the sun, making his task virtually impossible. One night, kneeling by his bed, he prayed, "Lord, please let there be tomatoes on my tomato plant tomorrow." The next morning he awoke, went outside, and saw huge, perfectly ripe, red tomatoes hanging from his plant. Donald was in awe— It was a miracle!

And then he looked a little closer. As he studied his miraculous tomato plant, he noticed little green pieces of wire that attached his tomatoes to the plant. And then it dawned on him: his mother had overheard his prayer, and in her desire to both bring him joy and encourage his faith, she bought some tomatoes from the local grocers and attached them to the plant while he slept. Two days later, the tomatoes were wrinkled, blackened, and quickly becoming rotten.

We should have learned by now that we cannot attach fake fruit to a living plant. Our job is not to create artificial fruit that makes our lives look great for a moment. Our calling instead is to nurture what God has entrusted to us. My role on Pais has always been to make sure it is healthy. All healthy things will eventually grow.

mall

Missionaries make missionaries. Pioneers produce pioneers.

Through the wonderful invention of social networking, I now hear stories on a daily basis of what our Pais missionaries are achieving around the world. It may be a tweet or a status update or even a video. Sometimes it's just a story. One of my favorites, although perhaps not the most dramatic, is of Adam and Lauren. While teaching about the Kingdom in the youth ministry they were involved in, and after unpacking how to truly disciple young people, Adam and Lauren came up with a plan.

Many have a misguided understanding of what discipleship is. Today it seems to be all about Christian education. At best, it is one-to-one in Starbucks… The Bible is opened, and then the one or two usually unnatural and always awkward accountability questions are asked. We have to remember those words…

Study how He did it.

When we do this, we realize that discipleship is, in fact, about taking people with us like Jesus did. Along the way, we will ask questions and so will they. Rather than teaching people, and then hoping they will go out and put into practice what we taught them in the classroom or over [insert your favorite Starbucks drink], we need to make them curious first.

So Adam and Lauren took the group of students they were discipling to a local mall to see the Kingdom come. The set study suggested eating dinner in the food court and then asking students the question, "If Jesus were here, what would He do?" The answer, they replied, was that He would demonstrate something of the nature of His Kingdom. So perhaps, they thought, we should tidy the food court for people. After doing this, the next question came: "How would

He demonstrate the Kingdom now?" The group pondered the question, then suggested that they could pay for someone's meal. "But who?" Perhaps the person most in need who could not return the favor... Maybe a single mother, they suggested. They noticed a woman with three children, so the members of the group cautiously made their way toward her. Just before they reached her, the woman picked up her phone and made a call.

The group patiently waited nearby.

When she finally put down her phone, she gathered her children around a table, sat down, and oddly put her head in her hands. The bravest member of the group tapped her on the shoulder and asked, "Excuse me, would you mind if we bought something for you and your family to eat?"

The woman's initial reaction was one of confusion and protest. "I can't afford to buy you anything," she said. After clearing up the misunderstanding and successfully communicating that they were offering to buy *her* food and not the other way round, the woman broke down in tears.

She confided that she was having a terrible day. Ten minutes earlier her purse had been stolen. A phone call to her husband had failed, and then she had panicked about how she would feed her children. It turned out she had gone to the school sponsored by the church that this youth group was from. The woman clearly saw that these students had been sent by God.

Just as importantly, this same fact began to dawn on the students themselves.

Missionaries making missionaries.

Adam and Lauren had not simply taught, but had helped young people experience God at work.

Now this story itself does not particularly create any testing problems for a pioneer; it's just a nice story of God using young people to train other even younger people. The fact is, however, it will lead to greater problems.

As you grow, so will those around you. They will get better at what they do. But they will require more space in which to do it. In the early days of pioneering, I had all the ideas. I had all the vision. The greatest challenge was to convince others. As time has passed, much of the vision of Pais has become based on the ideas of those growing up within it.

Now *they* have all the ideas, *they* have all the vision; the greatest challenge now is for *me* to be convinced.

Here is the danger: I give my authority to my leaders, they pass that authority on to their apprentices, their apprentices pass that authority on to those they mentor, and with every step, I lose a little bit of control. The pioneer's path becomes less predictable. It is now in the hands of those who carry your DNA.

Perhaps this is the greatest lesson you and I need to learn.

Ultimately, we pioneer not by passing on *control*, but by passing on *culture*.

Controls are dead, static, lifeless. Culture is alive. It is organic. It grows. It perpetuates its own growth by creating stories, both moving and comical, that are retold again and again by those within the movement, and these stories strengthen and add muscle to the culture. Pioneers continue to build Kingdom culture.

rachel e's story [gb]

I finished high school in Manchester with bucket loads of ambition but absolutely no idea about what I would do with my life. A friend of mine joined Pais the year before, and I remember laughing at the idea of someone working for free and following such strict rules and guidelines for a year. To my annoyance, as I finished my last year of college, I could not shake the idea that I was supposed to join the project as well.

It didn't take long, once I started working on the Pais team, to get my head around the fact that God had a lot more for me than I had ever realised. Surrounded by so many passionate and focused people, I soon caught the 'Missionaries Making

Missionaries' bug. Those first few years of Pais cemented in the core of my being that nothing would ever be more important than reaching people for God.

My second passion has always been drama, and I loved using it in school assemblies and lunchtime clubs. After two years on Pais, I considered leaving in order to study the Performing Arts further. However, God, and Paul Gibbs, had other plans. An idea to run a missional theatre company began to grow in my imagination and two days later, I received a call that would change the next five years of my life. 'Streetlevel' was a Christian theatre company running on the outskirts of London, and the manager was looking to Pais to take it forward. Within no time at all, I was driving south, feeling like I was living the dream that God had tailor-made for me. It was a phenomenal experience to work with other performers, touring schools around the whole of London. Pais taught me the power of imagination and confidence in God and His awesome plans. I had the great privilege of establishing a number of Pais' theatre companies around Britain and training other young adults under the auspices of the wider organisation.

Returning to sunny Manchester, I joined thefaithworks in Failsworth where I met my husband Steve who worked as a leader in the church and on the Eden Project. Together we established Create Performing Arts School with other Eden and youth workers. The aim of Eden was to build strong links with the local community, and Create became an ideal way to do this. Few creative projects for young people existed in the area, and so Create became very popular very quickly. Local police were extremely supportive, giving us a grant of £10,000[138] to help with start-up costs. Young people were soon learning drama, dance, singing, musical instruments, DJ-ing, and video editing in every room of the church. We ran a youth group after Create each week, and the vast majority of students stayed to learn about Jesus. We performed regularly at the church, reaching large numbers of young people, as well as their families and friends. There was nothing like the buzz of encouraging many young people in their creative gifting alongside their relationship with God. My personal motto became 'Unlocking Star Potential'; our aim was to raise a different breed of artist—not selfish, competitive, attention-seeking performers, but Godly, selfless, and highly committed creative young people. I will always be grateful for the opportunities that Pais gave me to create my own artis-

tic path, as well as for the way that I was supported through a part-time drama degree at university over the course of five years.

Even though I moved on from Pais to become a Drama Lecturer at a Further Education College, the impact of my seven years with Pais still remains with me. I found out what I was meant to do with my life and gained the confidence to follow the ideas that God has given to me. Even now, as I study a Masters Degree in Applied Theatre and seek to establish community theatre projects through the local church, I feel that I am building on everything that God began in me that day when I, timidly and apprehensively, went for my Pais interview in a cold office in Moston, Manchester. I am constantly reminded of this verse: 'Take delight in the Lord, and he will give you your heart's desires' (Psalm 37:4). I love the way that God creates and fulfills our hearts' desires!

I have already spoken in detail about Rachel in stage three of the book, but just to say again what fascinates me about God's work in young missionaries is their transformation in attitude and character. Rachel fought and won a battle: the battle of self. What made her unique was the blend of artistic personality and her selfless character. It was in this distinctive mix that we found a young woman who could lead people, many of which were older than her. There is nothing more wonderful than seeing someone you have released reproduce themselves in others and multiply the work of God's kingdom.

pete's story [gb]

I originally joined Pais just after I had finished my senior year exams. It was to be a one year experience before going to university. Nine years later I am still on Pais, having served as a team member, team leader, assistant course director, a member of the leadership team, and now National Director. Over the years, the most important thing I have learned is that the leaders who bring change to the world are those who care about character and integrity. It is the leaders who care about the little things as well as the big things.

In my journey, I have grown as Pais has. I have seen Pais in GB recruit apprentices from 15 different nations. I have watched the effectiveness of the schools that we impact increase as our vision has been redeveloped time and again. Over just the last few years, I have seen Pais plant teams in 50 different cities, towns, and villages, across churches of various denominations. Some teams have remained for years, and some have completed their task and moved on. A couple of years ago, we changed the way we measured success from one-time decisions to young people connected to churches that had previously not been. That year we saw well over 1000 young people integrated that had no prior church affiliation.

I have seen God work in some amazing ways on Pais, but like I say, it's also the little things that have excited me. Here are two of my favorite stories:

There was a girl called Titch (that wasn't her real name, but she was short and that's what her friends nicknamed her) who regularly came to our lunchtime event at her school. Every week we would have a prayer box available in which the students could ask for prayer for anything. At the end of the session we would take it back to our team office and pray for each request. A few weeks after Titch had put something in the prayer box she came up to me, pointing to a badge on her tie. It said 'Cancer Research'. I enquired about why she was wearing it, and she replied that she had asked us to pray for her grandmother who was dying of cancer. Days after she had put in the prayer request, she had heard that her grandmother had been given the all clear.

From 2000 to 2002 the Pais Burnley team I was on went into Barden Boys School to do assemblies and run a lunchtime event every Friday. We saw many boys from the school get connected with the youth ministry at Burnley Life Church (what was then Queensgate Pentecostal Church), become Christians, and get baptized. The best part of it? Several of the young men are now serving in the youth ministry, working in small groups in the community, and one of them has spent a year on Pais, reaching out to students who were in the same situation that he was just a few years before.

At 15 years old, as a brand new Christian, I had one ambition—to change the world! I had no idea what that meant or what was required but all I wanted was a chance. Pais gave me that opportunity by accepting me and placing me in Burnley. Almost a decade later, after working in several different locations, I have now returned to Burnley, seeking to make Great Britain great again, and serving in one of the best churches in the north of England.

In his book *Outliers*,[139] Malcolm Gladwell states that anybody who has made any significant impact in their sphere of influence has done so after 10,000 hours of practice. He goes on to say that it is not simply talent or ability, but approximately ten years of constant development that brings success. When I first met Pete, (I have to be honest) I instantly wrote him off, ironically because he looked just like Jesus. He had long black hair, a huge bushy beard, and piercing 'Hollywood Jesus' eyes. For some reason something about our initial conversation made me think he wasn't serious; how wrong could I have been? Pete is a testament to Gladwell's theory. Constantly learning, constantly improving, and constantly pushing himself outside of his comfort zone has made Pete one of the most respected Pais leaders in our short history and certainly there has never been anyone more likeable than him. We have often teased Pete that his biggest problem is that he's "nicer than Jesus". Approaching his tenth year, what motivates Pete, it seems to me, is a love for people not the system.

mawunyo's story [ghana]

I was working as the personal assistant of the General Overseer of Royalhouse Chapel International when a group of Americans visited Ghana to plan the construction of an orphanage as well as experience the culture. Wanting to serve, I decided to assist them throughout their trip, helping and driving them to their various mission locations. A member of the team who was experiencing Pais' success in their church encouraged me to join the ministry. After much prayer, I decided this was the right opportunity for me. I promised God that I was going to learn as much as possible, and then return home to impart all I had been taught into the lives of the young people of Africa.

In my first year on Pais I served in England in a small village, while in my second year I moved on to Pais:USA working directly under the leadership of Paul Gibbs. I spent hours in prayer both day and night, asking God to prepare me to help start the movement in Africa, so that young people could benefit from the strategy and teaching I'd seen in the West. I prayed for future apprentices, partnering churches, and financial supporters. It seemed a distant dream that Pais:Ghana was going to work as we had no funds available, but I kept remembering the word God had spoken to me: "Go and do it because I will use you to change many lives and transform many people on the continent of Africa."

REPRODUCTION || YOUR STORY

As the American school year finished, I embarked on a 21-day fast, praying and committing what I was going to start in my own nation into God's hands. Immediately after the fast, my pastor visited me in Texas and confirmed that my home church would partner with the Pais Project and would provide all we needed to start in Africa—this was the breakthrough I desired.

Pais:Ghana started with a team of three—myself and two first year apprentices, one from Germany and one from America. We started by going into three schools, but Pais strategies proved successful, and at the end of the year we were in five. As well as reaching out in rural areas seeing thousands saved, we visited other churches, training them in Pais' style of youth ministry.

I continued to pray for bigger things, and our second year intake saw us grow to two teams with ten apprentices, the majority being from Africa, serving within eight schools. We served the neighboring remote areas with compassion ministry, helping with both spiritual and physical needs. Our aim was also to train local people in the new methods and philosophies I had learned.

During these first years, on one particular trip to a remote part of the Volta region we had a special encounter. A local pastor had apparently received a vision of a photocopier. He felt that God had told him that he was to reproduce something, but he was left confused by the image in his mind. When our team began to serve in the area, everything clicked. He believed God was telling him to photocopy the Pais team. A few months later Paul Gibbs was due to speak at a conference in Accra and the two leaders of this fledgling team travelled through the night to receive training from him. I think Paul was a little surprised to find he had a part-time team of twelve he never knew about.

My dream is to spread our vision into other African nations in the coming years. We are already beginning to receive applicants from other African nations and interest from churches in Ghana's bordering countries. I am anticipating God's moving and our work becoming an instrument within the entire African continent, affecting millions of young lives.

Mawunyo's story is only just beginning. I am keeping a special eye on what happens in Africa. It's perhaps the most unpredictable Pais nation so far. I was surprised, delighted, and stunned on my first visit to meet the team that travelled through the night from the jungle of the Volta region. The team was led by a young border patrol policeman called Edward. Pais does not believe in franchises, and so we began the process of making this team fully Pais. But it is such a great example of how, after many battles, suddenly and for no apparent reason, there is a cataclysmic effect and things multiply so quickly.

Pioneer, this will happen to you.

barbs

Pioneers are living stones.

Any bricklayer knows that to build a solid building, one stone must be put on top of another. As a pioneer you will feel 'put on'. In fact, that's your role.

In the introduction to this book, we conjured up the image of a brave soldier throwing himself over a wall of barbed wire in order that his band of brothers can walk over him and take their enemy's position.

These barbs cut into us. They can cause us pain. They can disfigure us.

I have a good friend whom I have come to respect more and more over the years. Mark was born with an innate gift to make people laugh and communicate his thoughts. This led to him being a hugely successful public speaker. His calendar is constantly booked. He is courted by the largest conferences, churches, and platforms in his nation.

He is, without doubt, a success.

Mark's ultimate desire is to connect people with a message of his faith. He is one of the most passionate people I know. When something stays motivated by love, it inevitably becomes creative. The more successful Mark has become in the eyes of his friends and colleagues, the more he has actually questioned the worth and effectiveness of what he does.

Some of *his* awkward questions are:

> *Am I preaching to the choir?*
> *Have I become a tourist attraction for Christians?*
> *Is this the best way I can use my natural gifts?*

In his own estimation, although Mark was speaking to thousands, only the very fringe were his real audience, the ones he felt called and destined to connect with...those he refers to as "going to a forever without God". That's a heartbreaking conclusion to come to: that although everyone else wishes they were you, you wish you were someone else.

In Mark's case, he was someone who recognized it was not the healthy who needed a doctor, but the sick. Someone called not to the righteous but to the sinners of the world.[140]

Mark had a revelation.[141]

Instead of making his living from touring churches and Christian conferences, speaking to large numbers of the choir but only handfuls of the fringe, he would find a different platform. He would create a comedy tour. Booking small theatres that could hold just a few hundred, he created a one hour performance where he shared three adventures in his life, the third being a spiritual one. It was much riskier. It meant saying "no" to the meat and potatoes of what he traditionally did. As I write, Mark is in the pioneering stages. It is beginning to take off. A DVD is being produced. Most importantly, the vast majority of those who come out to hear him do not go to church and have probably never heard a message anything like the one Mark speaks. But there are several barbs he will need to throw himself onto.

A few months ago I had the privilege of hearing my friend unpack a little bit more of his dream. He painted the picture of standing on stage in the major theatres of Britain and across the world. In my mind, he certainly has the gifting and talent to pull this off. Instead of reaching hundreds, he would speak to thousands upon thousands. Towards the end of our conversation, I felt prompted to ask him a question.

Invoking an understanding of the fourth stage of pioneering, I inquired, "What if you are the pioneer, and God uses you to create a new way, but then someone else comes along after all your hard work, and it is that person who tours the larger centers of the entertainment world?"

It is a question I have to ask myself.

It is not a rule of the four processes that the pioneer will never be the one to become famous for creating the new way. It is, however, a possibility—a possibility that you need to come to peace with in order to pass the final test of pioneering.

When we first came to America, one person said to me, "Paul, you have to be careful about sharing the idea of Pais. The economic model is so compelling, the concept is so thrilling, and the implementation is so effective that someone else with much more resources may come along and steal the idea."

Yes...and so what?

Pioneer, let me encourage you to ask yourself that question before you walk the path. You need to come to a place of peace with a possible scenario that you may end your life as a bloody, trampled corpse, with barbs in your belly and footprints on your back, lying on a field that has long since been forgotten.

A pioneer does not just make a way. He becomes the way.

To be forewarned is to be forearmed.

REPRODUCTION || YOUR STORY

questions for the pioneer

1. Can you relate to the Matador Vine?

2. Why do you think it's easier to put tomatoes on a plant than make the plant healthy enough to grow its own?

3. Pioneering means to lie on barbed wire. Which barbs are you prepared to suffer?

EPILOGUE

EPILOGUE

glass

Sometimes, fact is stranger than fiction.

According to a press release by Reuters some time back, Israel's National Park Authority approved plans for perhaps the world's most bizarre tourist attraction.

Jutting out from the beach, a submerged walkway in the Sea of Galilee at Capernaum was designed so that tourists can "walk on water" where Jesus reputedly did 2,000 years ago. Apparently since the walkway would not have a railing, it was decided that lifeguards in rescue boats would be nearby to save people from drowning.

The walkway would be made of glass.

It was designed to be invisible.

Transparent.

I am guessing that the point is simple. Tourists can stroll along the attraction pretending to walk on water. Their friends can take photographs and video clips. YouTube, Facebook, and various other online sites will be able to catalogue their acts of faith.

Of course, they are not really walking on water. They are not really acting by faith. Something else is holding them up that is invisible to the natural eye.

Many of us want to make a difference in the world—to live a life of significance. Yet many of us also want those invisible supports.

Perhaps the process of pioneering in the Kingdom is all about God carefully dismantling the glass walkway below us.

This book does not aim to make you famous or grow your business or church or organization. It is a call out for those who want to pioneer for the purest of motives...for God's motive. Dismantling the tourist attraction in our lives can give us this one true motive. True Kingdom pioneers go beyond selfish ambitions that lie deep within all of us, especially me.

EPILOGUE

They advance through all four stages of Kingdom Pioneering:

> They seek a **revelation** although they may feel alone.
>
> They cause a **revolution** and may be seen as a threat.
>
> They continue to **resist** the temptation to compromise their uniqueness.
>
> They desire to **reproduce** themselves by giving their authority away.

This book is part of the Kingdom Trilogy, three books that propose an alternative way to advance the Kingdom of God.

Why alternative?

In the case of *The Line and the Dot,* this going of the extra mile, we have looked at the alternative to how many people hope to see the Kingdom come. Many are looking for a risk-free, already proven, method of success.

Their glass walkway is their security.

Many things provide that security for them: a successful economic model, a title that gives a certain status, a consensus of opinion that makes them feel validated...the list goes on.

We do not need a new kind of *program*. We need a new kind of *person*.

For those of you who have given up hope that the Kingdom can be advanced in your life, your community, and your world, take note.

All things are possible when you go beyond yourself...when you go further than what is required.

You will walk off the glass walkway, and so far beyond the line, that when you look back, you will see...

The line has become a mere dot.

END NOTES

THE LINE AND THE DOT — END NOTES

Prologue

1. The only time Jesus mentioned crosses are those that we as his disciples have to bear (Luke 14:27).
2. In Jesus' day the Tetragrammaton - YHWH could only be uttered in the Temple, in the daily blessing and confession of the high priest on the day of atonement according to the oral law Sifre Numbers 39; Sotah 7:6m. Yoma 6:2
3. Strong's Greek Lexicon entry 932 - 'Basileia'
4. Matthew 5:38-48
5. Matthew 19:12

Introduction | The Spirit of the Pioneer

6. Hebrews 12:1-3 [The Message]
7. Merriam-Webster entry for 'pioneer'
8. Matthew 11:12
9. For some interesting insight into this, see <u>The Sage from Galilee</u> by Professor David Flusser, p.31. Flusser, David with R. Steven Notely. <u>The Sage from Galilee</u>. Michigan: WM. D. Earmans Publishing Company, 2007.
10. It actually used his surname, but for obvious reasons I will not include it.
11. Taylor, J.Hudson. <u>Hudson Taylor (Man of Faith).</u> Ada, MI: Bethany House, 1987.
12. Pullinger, Jackie. <u>Chasing the Dragon: One Woman's Struggle against the Darkness of Hong Kong's Drug Dens.</u> Ventura, CA: Regal Book, 2007.
13. Cunningham, Loren. <u>Is That Really You, God?</u> Seattle: YWAM Publishers, 2001.
14. For those science nerds among you, find out more at Wikipedia's entry for 'Pioneer 10'.
15. Martin Luther King, Jr., Washington, DC, August 28th, 1963, during the march on Washington.
16. Winston Churchill, during the Battle of Britain, August 20th, 1940.
17. Jesus Christ, John 14:6
18. Ephesians 6:10-11

END NOTES

Stage One | Revelation | My Story

19 Paul was one of the local church ministers who had previously reached into local schools. He was an evangelist in the true sense of the word; not only did he spread the word of Jesus, he equipped the people of God and generously passed on all that he had known. Paul was such an inspiration to me that for a while I thought maybe I was called to be an evangelist as well. I realized that was not to be the case, but some of the simple tools that Paul gave me during that time, I still use today. I thank God for men like Paul whose influence goes far beyond the people they can physically see or touch. To learn more about him, visit www.paulandchristinemorley.com.

Stage One | Revelation | Our Story

20 Matthew 3:13-16

21 Damon Hill first became a Formula One racing driver with Williams F1 Team in 1992. He won the championship in 1996, and retired in 1999. For more information, check out his entry on Wikipedia.

22 "Fix your eyes on Jesus the author and perfecter of our faith" – Hebrews 12:2 (The Message)

23 Hebrews 12:2 (The Message)

24 Luke 18:38; Mark 10:47

25 Acts 9:4-5

26 Luke 2:41-46

27 Oneighty is the 7th-12th grade ministry of Church On The Move located in Tulsa, Oklahoma.

Stage One | Revelation | Your Story

28 Luke 2:47-50

29 Jewish tradition says that this was Moses; however, nothing in the book confirms that he was the author. Check your Bible commentary for details.

30 See the book of Job chapters 1 and 2 in the Bible.

31 In a future book, I want to explain how Judaism changed between the Old and the New Testaments. The blank page that many of us have in our Bibles represents four to five hundred years of profound philosophical and moral discussion. We cannot fully understand the teaching of Jesus when we are ignorant of the context of His teaching. But that, as I say, is for another book and without that insight, we have to understand that Job's friends were in the same situation as many Christians today.

32	At the time of writing, that was about $75 dollars. What was great about this was that even though the church I was part of was so small, the pastor Harry Letson, a great man of God, believed in me so much that he took a cut in his wages in order for me to receive this money.
33	All are located in Philadelphia, PA, USA.
34	Merriam-Webster entry for 'pioneer'.
35	Merriam-Webster entry for 'radical'.

Stage Two | Revolution | My Story

36	Quote from Joe Hayes, a pastor from Manchester, England, reflecting on his Pais experiences.
37	Luke 5:4-7
38	You can read more about this at www.fishingtheabyss.com

Stage Two | Revolution | Our Story

39	Matthew 12:1-2
40	Genesis 1:1
41	1 John 4:8
42	Mishnah Tractate Avot. Chapter 1. Verse 1.
43	Survey taken by the International Bible Society.
44	Mark 9:38-40
45	Jefferson, Thomas (1802-01-01). "Jefferson's Letter to the Danbury Baptists". U.S. Library of Congress.
46	Matthew 13:24-29
47	Definition entry for 'weeds'. Stern, David H. <u>Jewish New Testament Commentary.</u> Baltimore: Jewish New Testament Publicatons, Inc., 1992.
48	The Jewish New Testament Commentary notes that in the gospel of Mark that those who are not with Jesus were seen to be against Him and that the Pharisees that Jesus is addressing had come to their final opportunity. It was their last chance, and if at their last chance they were not for Him, they were seen to be against Him.
49	Mishnah Tractate Avot. Chapter 1. Verse 1.
50	Exodus 20:8
51	Matthew 12:9-14
52	Mark 7:8
53	Mark 7:9

END NOTES

54   Gass, Bob. 'Word For Today': *Date unknown*
55   Luke 18:9-14
56   Exodus 20:7 (Taken from the New King James Version)

Stage Two | Revolution | Your Story

57   Matthew 12:1-8
58   Matthew 10:26
59   Proverbs 4:23
60   Romans 5:6-8
61   Coca-Cola CEO Donald R. Keough, "Passion: Life's Single Most Important Ingredient," Commencement address, Emory University, May 10, 1993.
62   Dr. Merrill Douglass, in *Homemade*, April, 1990.
63   Ephesians 6:12
64   Matthew 5:39
65   For a greater understanding of Jesus' illustration and its basis in competition, not conflict, see pg. 209-210 'Meet the Rabbis' – Brad Young.

Stage Three | Resistance | My Story

66   'Talmidim' is a Hebrew word meaning 'disciples'. The singular version, disciple, is translated *talmid*.
67   Approximately $279,000
68   Approximately $75,000
69   Joseph Joubert, French Essayist and Moralist (1754-1824)
70   Before they fully understood He was God, they may have initially believed He was a good rabbi to follow; some may have understood He was the Messiah.
71   Rick Warren, partially quoting former US president Harry S. Truman in The Purpose Driven Church. Warren, Rick. The Purpose Driven Church: Growth Without Compromising Your Message & Mission. Grand Rapids: Zondervan, 1995.
72   Acts 8:18-20
73   'Church? No Thanks.' Why Teens are leaving in droves. Grace, Rebecca. AFA Journal, May 2008.
74   1 Samuel 17:39
75   1 Samuel 17:36
76   Talmud, Kesuvos 5a

Stage Three | Resistance | Our Story

77. John 6:14-15
78. There is a reason for this that I will discuss in the third book of this trilogy about Kingdom Patterns.
79. Isaiah 9:1-2
80. In fact, a Roman mile marker designating this route can still be seen today in Capernaum's ruins.
81. John 1:43-44
82. Nelson Illustrated Bible Dictionary. It is also an important fact that most of His disciples were from the area. Nelson states that all of the twelve, with exception of Judas, came from the area. However, one ancient document, alluded to by early writers as the Gospel of the Ebionites, even states that Judas was from the Galilee. This seems to verify what the New Testament says in Acts 1:11 and 2:7, where the disciples were addressed as "men of Galilee" and "Galileans".
83. Ray Vander Laan, see endnote 135.
84. Even today, there are stories of orthodox Jews whose disciples follow them into the restroom to gain insight on the right way to use the facility.
85. Matthew 11:30

Stage Three | Resistance | Your Story

86. Matthew 4:1-11
87. For more background and interesting insights into the origins of some of our modern day practices, take a look at *Pagan Christianity* by Frank Viola and George Barna.
88. Matthew 28:19
89. Encarta Online Encyclopedia
90. Matthew 6:24
91. To 'Look a gift horse in the mouth' is a figurative expression meaning to question the gift or gift-giver, to be ungrateful to someone who gives you something, or to treat the gift-giver badly. Here, it is intended to mean 'question the gift'.
92. Matthew 6:31
93. This was a quote in one of the major national tabloids in England. To emphasize their point, the reporters from this particular newspaper also pointed out that some of the teenagers had never seen a cow.
94. Approximately $3,250
95. Approximately $19,500

END NOTES

96   Approximately $26,000
97   Approximately $101,000
98   Luke 9:51
99   Matthew 12:28
100   Luke 9:60
101   John 6:66
102   Mark 8:38
103   Matthew 21:11-14
104   Matthew 6:15
105   Matthew 27:37
106   This happened when Jesus was probably between the ages of 8 and 10 years old. Judas the Galilean had led a revolt against the Romans but, when Rome responded, the rebels were crucified and many women and children sold into slavery.
107   Approximately $6500
108   Acts 16:10
109   Mishnah Bava Metsi'a 2:11
110   Mishnah Bava Metsi'a 2:11
111   Luke 14:26
112   Matthew 10:37-38
113   To read just how this happened, take a look at John 6:53-66

Stage Four | Reproduction | My Story

114   John 12:24
115   Psalm 127:1-2
116   Psalm 127:3-5
117   To see a short video of Teaching Pastor Max Lucado speak about the Pais teams' input at his church in San Antonio, Texas, go to www.paisproject.com
118   2 Kings 13:14
119   2 Kings 13:15-17
120   Freeman, James M. <u>Manners and Customs of the Bible,</u> New York: Logos International (from original printing of Nelson & Philips), 1972. Page 179.
121   2 Kings 12:18-19

THE LINE AND THE DOT ⋯ END NOTES

Stage Four | Reproduction | Our Story

122   Swampy's real name was the very conservative sounding Daniel Hooper.

123   Matthew 10:38-39

124   Acts 2:43-47

125   John 14:12

126   Jaqueline L. Salmon, October 8th 2008, *Pew Maps Muslim Populations Worldwide*, The Washington Post Online.

127   Taken from a speech by Roddick at the Academy of Management, Vancouver, August 1995.

128   *Quote from Anita Roddick*

129   1999 vote by the Consumers Association

130   On March 17, 2006, Roddick sold The Body Shop for £652 million, causing all manner of controversies since L'Oreal (the buyer) tests its products on animals. Had Roddick injected a Trojan horse as she hoped into one of the conglomerates of the world, or had she succumbed bizarrely to the third test of a pioneer? Only time will tell. What we do know is that she died eighteen months later on September 10, 2007.

131   Isaiah 54:2

132   Matthew 5:13

Stage Four | Reproduction | Your Story

133   'Matador Vine' is one of the common names of the Bladderflower [*Araujia sericifera*] – also referred to as the 'cruel plant.'

134   Matthew 16:16-19

135   Ray Vander Laan is an excellent teacher whose lectures are published by Zondervan.

136   <u>Developing the Leader Within You</u> and <u>Developing the Leaders Around You</u> by John Maxwell are hugely affirming books for pioneers who want to make it all the way through the four stages of a Kingdom pioneer. I recommend them to you. (Nashville: Thomas Nelson Publishing, 2005)

137   Hebrews 12:1-2 (The Message)

138   Approximately $16,500

139   Gladwell, Malcolm. <u>Outliers: The Story of Success.</u> Boston: Little, Brown and Company, 2008.

140   Mark 2:17 (paraphrased)

141   Mark is currently touring with his own one man evangelistic theatre show, mixing his unique blend of humor with the Gospel message. For more information visit www.73rdtrust.com.

about the kingdom trilogy

the line and the dot

the first in the trilogy, this book studies kingdom pioneering.

using the motif of a pioneer, it presents an alternative view of *vision* in the kingdom of God.

the cloud and the line

the second in the trilogy, this book examines kingdom principles.

using the motif of a knight, it presents an alternative view of *morality* in the kingdom of God.

the seed and the cloud

the third in the trilogy, this book analyzes kingdom patterns.

using the motif of a pilgrim, it presents an alternative view of *guidance* in the kingdom of God.

www.facebook.com/thelineandthedot
www.facebook.com/thecloudandtheline
www.facebook.com/theseedandthecloud

about the author

paul gibbs is the founding & global director of pais. he is married to lynn and has two sons, joel and levi. originally from manchester, england, paul moved to the usa in 2005.

paul began pioneering openings into manchester schools as an associate minister in 1987. in september 1992 he founded the pais project. initially a vision for a one-team gap year project in north manchester, the project has exploded globally, training and placing thousands of missionaries and reaching millions of students throughout europe, north america, asia, and africa.

while continuing to direct pais, paul has served in various other roles: director with youth alive [uk]; senior minister at thefaithworks [uk] where he launched a mentoring academy; and as a senior leader at pantego bible church [tx, usa].

paul founded global:pais, the international resource team for pais throughout the world. this team continues to grow and has since launched initiatives such as www.mypais.info, livewire online training, and other resources.

paul gained national recognition in the uk for mentoring and training leaders. he has written courses for and spoken at various bible colleges and seminaries in the uk and the states, including mattersey bible college [uk], nazarene theological college [uk], and southwestern baptist theological seminary [tx, usa].

teaching throughout the world, his primary topics include pioneering, leadership development, the kingdom of God, and ancient practices for post-modern times.

paul enjoys swimming, surfing, skiing, sailing, snowboarding, and is an avid manchester united fan!

find out more at
www.paul-gibbs.info
www.facebook.com/paulcgibbs
www.twitter.com/paulcgibbs

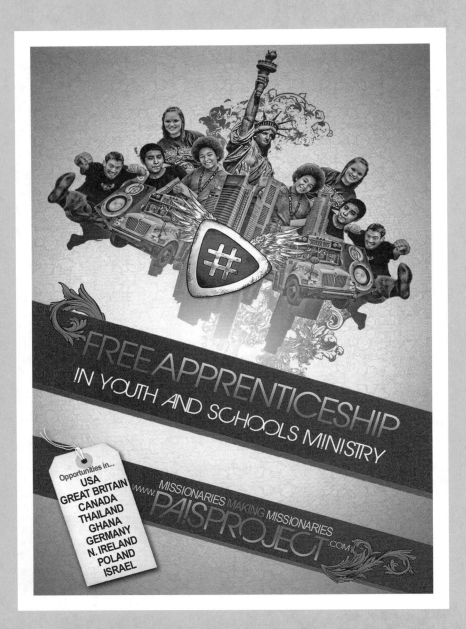

about the pais project

our aim

to spark a global movement in schools by empowering churches with kingdom-minded apprentices who serve in youth ministry and work in local schools, building relational bridges between the two.

our motto

missionaries making missionaries

our passion

we are passionate about the young people of our world and are desperate to see them in the relationship with God that He intended us to have. always appreciative of the school's policies and sensitive to their needs, we assist them as they seek to help young people find their purpose. we come alongside the vision of the local church and endeavour to empower the youth as they grow in their understanding and experience of God.

our name

pais is the new testament greek word for child or child servant to the king.

our vision is to take the young people we disciple and help them become all they can be.

mission lies at the heart of pais. we don't see it as a one-time event, but seek to help both the apprentice and those they touch to develop a missionary heart, missionary skills, and a missionary life. as each missionary makes a missionary, we see our world change.

our details:
www.paisproject.com
www.facebook.com/paisproject
www.twitter.com/paisproject

Pais is about equipping churches with kingdom-minded apprentices, who relationally reach out to the young people in the schools they work in.

M!SS!ONARY MAKERS

Pais Scholarships are an intentional way for you to help support the work of Pais throughout the world. Each scholarship allows us to plant an apprentice or a team of apprentices in one of the following nations:

GB NORTHERN IRELAND GERMANY USA CANADA GHANA POLAND ISRAEL EIRE INDIA BRAZIL

 Apprentice Scholarship
$2,500 enables us to **RECRUIT, TRAIN, MENTOR & MOBILIZE** a full-time Pais Missionary for an entire year.

 Team Scholarship
$10,000 enables us to **RECRUIT, TRAIN, MENTOR & MOBILIZE** a Pais Team in a new city for an entire year.

For more information contact globalpais@paisproject.com

PA!SPROJECT
www.paisproject.com

about partnering with the pais project

scholarships

pais scholarships provide an intentional strategy enabling you to support the work of the pais project throughout the world. scholarships are a way for us to put great role models into schools and build relational bridges with them into faith-based communities.

apprentice scholarship

$2,500 enables us to recruit, train, mentor, and mobilize a full-time pais missionary for an entire year.

team scholarship

$10,000 enables us to recruit, train, mentor, and mobilize a full-time pais team in a new city for an entire year.

three ways you can help

you could provide part of a scholarship

you could provide one or more scholarships

you could gather a group or team to raise one or more scholarships

contact

globalpais@paisproject.com
www.paisproject.com
www.facebook.com/paisproject